The Opium Wars

Exploring the Addiction of Empires
from Beginning to End

Adrian Ramos, **History** Compacted

Copyright © 2019 by Sea Vision Publishing, LLC

All Rights Reserved.

No part of this publication may be reproduced, distributed, or transmitted in any form or by any means, including photocopying, recording, electronic or mechanical methods, without the prior written permission of the publisher, except in the case of brief quotations embodied in critical reviews and certain other non-commercial uses permitted by copyright law.

Much research, from a variety of sources, has gone into the compilation of this material. We strive to keep the information up-to-date to the best knowledge of the author and publisher; the materials contained herein is factually correct. Neither the publisher nor author will be held responsible for any inaccuracies.

ISBN: 9781702160032

Table of Contents

Table of Contents *3*

A Note From History Compacted *7*

Introduction The Slow Burn *9*

Chapter One The Opium Trade up to 1799 .... *13*

    What is Opium? 13

    The History of Opium in China 15

    European Addictions 17

    American Silver, Chinese Coffers 19

    The Canton System & Fallout of the Flint Affair 23

Chapter Two The Opium Trade from 1800-1838 .... *26*

    Floating Warehouses 26

    The White Lotus Rebellion 28

    The Foreign Quarter 30

    Diplomatic Blunders & Insults 33

    Lin & Elliot Enter the Scene 37

    Flashpoint at Kowloon 43

Chapter Three The First Opium War, 1839-1842 .... *47*

    The Battle of Kowloon 47

The First Battle of Chuenpi	50
Declaration of War	53
The Palmerston Letters	57
Mobilization	59
Inroads to China	62
The Convention of Chuenpi	65
Fighting Upriver	67
The Battles of Canton	70
North to Amoy	75
Ningbo & How to Loot It	77
The Yangtze River Campaign	80
The Treaty of Nanking	84
Chapter Four The Interwar Period, 1842-1856	*88*
Anti-Manchuism	88
The Taiping Rebellion	91
European Resentment	94
The Arrow Incident	96
Chapter Five The Second Opium War, 1856-1860	*99*
British Escalation	99
France Wades In	101
Another Battle of Canton	103
Capitulation at Taku & the Treaties of Tianjin	106

- Return to Hostilities & the Second Battle of Taku Forts.... 110
- Third Battle of Taku Forts 113
- The Road to Peking.. 115
- The War Ends 117

Chapter Six Aftermath *119*
- The Convention of Peking 119
- Post-War China 121
- The Future of Opium 123

Conclusion.. *126*

References *128*

About History Compacted *135*

Dark Minds In History... *137*

A Note
From History Compacted

Hi there!

This is Jason Chen, founder of History Compacted. Before you continue your journey to the past, I want to take a quick moment to explain our position on history and the purpose of our books.

To us, history is more than just facts, dates, and names. We see history as pieces of stories that led to the world we know today. Besides, it makes it much more fun seeing it that way too.

That is why History Compacted was created: to tell amazing stories of the past and hopefully inspire you to search for more. After all, history would be too big for any one book. But what each book can give you is a piece of the puzzle to help you get to that fuller picture.

Lastly, I want to acknowledge the fact that history is often told from different perspectives. Depending on the topic and your upbringing, you might agree or disagree with how we present the facts. I understand disagreements are inevitable. That is why with a team of diverse writers, we aim to tell each story from a more neutral perspective. I hope this note can help you better understand our position and goals.

Now without further ado, let your journey to the past begin!

Introduction

The Slow Burn

The year is 1810 CE, and in the bustling southern Chinese port city of Canton, the harbors are dense with galleons and merchant junks, the streets crowded with millions of people.

Above it all stand enormous factory buildings. For almost two hundred years, the dynasty of the Great Qing has ruled Imperial China and its cities, such as Canton.

Founded by invading Manchus from Northeast Asia during the death throes of the Ming Dynasty in the seventeenth century, this vast empire is now the powerhouse of East Asia.

The reign of the previous emperor Qianlong allowed China to enter into a new golden age, where it pacified the frontier tribes and subjugated its neighbors, while crushing countless rebellions. It has commercialized, urbanized, and modernized China into the largest economy by GDP in the world. The markets of coastal cities are drowning in silver.

But there is decay under all this grandeur. Resentment festers among dissidents, rivals, and downtrodden minority groups. Corrupt government officials enrich themselves.

Foreign powers from overseas carve out larger and less equal trade deals. And in those same coastal markets, in Canton and elsewhere, something far more sinister than silver is flooding in: opium.

This powerful, addictive narcotic has people of all classes and all walks of life in its grip; ruining lives and putting a huge strain on China's resources.

Its presence in the city is an open secret. One doesn't have to walk far or search hard to find a hazy opium den full of people reclining on couches in dreamlike stupors.

The reigning Jiaqing Emperor ruling from Peking far in the north issues yet another decree reminding the empire that opium is and has been illegal for decades. Once again, he calls for the destruction of this poison, and the arrest of its merchants and smugglers. But another imperial degree will do little to slow imports. The lives of farmers depend on it, and the tax system would be crippled without it. The Europeans watching and waiting from offshore with their huge batteries of guns would be displeased by it.

Opium, and the trade wars, which will be fought for and against it, will hammer the first nail in to the coffin of Imperial China.

Chapter One

The Opium Trade up to 1799

What is Opium?

It is difficult to understand the chaos and near-total collapse of social order caused by the Opium Wars without knowing what the drug is, and the level of human suffering it caused.

Opium is made from the latex—a sticky, milky secretion like sap or resin—of the poppy plant *Papaver somniferum*. Not all poppy varieties produce opium, and they have many uses other than their latex. The opium poppy is grown across the world today, but historically was limited to Mediterranean Europe and West or South Asia. It contains an analgesic alkaloid compound called morphine, which is a powerful narcotic substance.

Today, a huge variety of drugs are made by extracting the morphine from opium and refining it into different forms. This is how heroin is made, as well as many pain killers. But for much of history opium was consumed in a raw, unrefined form, often by vaporizing and inhaling it through a special pipe.

Taking opium greatly reduces pain and can cause drowsiness, a feeling of euphoria or detachment, shallowness of breath, and constipation. Long-term abuse can cause dependence, lung edema, and respiratory or cardiac collapse. Even controlled use for medicinal purposes can lead to addiction. Withdrawal effects can be almost as lethal as the drug itself.

In a time and place before modern medicine and rehabilitation—like many areas of nineteenth century China—opium addicts were usually customers for life. Those lives were normally short and painful as a result. And for the opium dealers and smugglers who witnessed this, it was terribly easy to be blinded by the money it made.

It is difficult to understate the damage greed and opium caused to people and communities in this time period, like they do today. And it is vital to keep this in mind as one reads ahead, so that the tragic spiral China and its European associates were trapped in can be understood.

The History of Opium in China

The milky extract of the poppy plant was known to China long before it flooded the markets during the late Qing period. It was first known during the Tang Dynasty of the seventh to tenth centuries, having been brought east by Arab traders. For centuries it was known by names like yingsu soup or black spice.

It was mostly limited to religious or medical purposes at first. Daoists believed it could help regulate chi, while doctors saw it as a cure for diarrhea or as a way to enhance sexual health and ability in men and women. By the end of the Ming Dynasty in 1637, it had acquired a reputation as an aphrodisiac used to prolong arousal in elaborate or long-lasting sexual acts.

Considering what it would do in later days, it might be surprising that opium remained legal and mostly unregulated in China for hundreds of years. The substance slowly gained a wide enough appeal beyond ritual uses to be made a taxable commodity.

To the late Ming royalty it was even valuable enough to be part of the Chinese tributary system. Hundreds of pounds of opium were offered as gifts to Ming emperors by the Siamese Kingdom of Ayutthaya in modern day Thailand, alongside other rare and exotic goods like frankincense, ivory, and peacock feathers.

When the Ming fell to civil war and invading Manchus became the ruling class of a new Qing Dynasty, the mystique and allure of opium survived among the Han Chinese elite. It eventually spread to their Manchu lords, which allowed opium use to survive for decades as a leisurely activity of the wealthy and powerful.

Political relationships with other kingdoms in South and Southeast Asia shifted and changed over the generations, but the cultural exchange started by the Ming tributary system guaranteed that certain practices would be shared with China.

This included the recreational smoking of madak—a blend of tobacco and opium. Smoking madak had been already popular among Siamese, Javanese, and Bengali commoners for centuries. Members of the Chinese diaspora living in port cities like Batam and Batavia—modern day Jakarta, Java—

picked up this habit by the early eighteenth century. In turn, it was spread to the common people of Qing.

But the recreational use of opium by common folk tarnished its former reputation as a mystical, sensual thing of the upper class, and finally revealed how destructive it could be to society. The Yongzheng Emperor criminalized madak in 1729, and subsequent emperors would continue to take minor actions against the drug.

Opium continued to enter China in many forms. Local dealers would buy opium from smugglers and distribute it to the many drug dens in port cities and beyond. This created a small but growing smuggling industry and black market.

European Addictions

This trend didn't go unnoticed by outsiders. Thanks to hundreds of years of imperialist ambition, the port cities of those Siamese, Javanese, and Bengali people who were in contact with the Chinese were often under the control of Europeans.

Merchant groups and colonies like the British East India Company and the Dutch East Indies already had firm control of parts of the Indian Subcontinent and Southeast Asia by the seventeenth century. They were also no strangers to exploiting local markets for profits back home. These early European capitalists saw the potential for a much larger market for opium in mainland China, and decided to make it a reality.

The Portuguese were the first to try selling opium to China, exporting it from Indian ports like Goa and Daman. Next came the British through their East India Company (EIC), which by 1773, controlled huge swaths of India and Bengal.

The EIC tried to form a monopoly on the opium trade after conquering opium-producing parts of the shrinking Mughal Dynasty. The EIC was deep in debt thanks to its wars with the Mughals and other powers in India, so peddling the drug to China seemed like a good way to start turning a profit again. By 1793, dominating the opium market and eyeing markets in China was an explicit part of the EIC's charter.

But there was a deeper desire—a deeper need—fueling the English, Portuguese, and other ambitious Europeans in Asia.

The Western powers which were becoming more and more interested in the opium market in China, had already been dealing with their own obsessions for generations. But opium wasn't their drug. Their addiction was to silk, porcelain, and tea.

The wealthy consumers of early modern Europe and the Americas got a taste of fine Chinese goods like silk, porcelain, and tea early on in the Age of Exploration. But European markets lacked the ability to manufacture those luxury goods as well or as fast as the Chinese could.

So they remained limited to buying them from China, often at a steep price. But the desire for these goods only grew, and so did the cost to afford them. This might not have been so bad for westerners, if not for the fact that the only accepted form of payment for all these goods was the increasingly limited resource of silver.

American Silver, Chinese Coffers

The global circulation of silver had been transformed in the last three hundred years, thanks to the so-called Columbian Exchange and the exploitation of people and natural resources in the Americas.

The early Spanish Conquistadors and Portuguese explorers had gotten a taste for American gold and silver after so much of it had been looted from the cities of the Aztecs, Maya, and Inca.

When there was no more to be taken, the Spanish used the expertise of local Native Americans to mine more from the mountains of Central and South America. When the indigenous people were devastated by disease and mistreatment, their colonial masters brought in slaves from West Africa to replace them. These laborers toiled away thanklessly, digging in the darkness of mine shafts or processing silver ore using noxious and sometimes poisonous materials like mercury.

The net result of this besides unimaginable human suffering was a whole lot of precious metal entering circulation across the world. From 1560 to 1685 between twenty-five thousand to thirty thousand tons of silver were produced by the mines of New Spain.

From 1686 to 1810, that amount more than doubled. The small, formerly poor kingdoms of the Iberian Peninsula became very rich, very fast, and it didn't take long before that silver began to flow in to other European nations with goods to sell.

At the same time, the Qing Dynasty was coming into its own, and China was slowly opening itself back up to international trade the way it hadn't since the later years of the Ming. It still wasn't much, however, because the Middle Kingdom prided itself in being self-sufficient and avoiding dependency on foreign imports. And it just so happened that China was very good at being self-sufficient, because of how huge and diverse its economy was.

The one exception to this was silver, which China was happy to accept as a form of payment. This is because Chinese currency was backed by and made of silver, which couldn't easily be mined in China. Because it was literally currency, any silver imported from abroad expanded the Chinese money supply. This led to Chinese markets growing and becoming more competitive with the rest of the world, while also staying fairly stable.

Flushed with silver from the Americas, Europeans were finally able to offer China its most desired payment for silk, tea, and manufactured goods. And for a time, things were good. China grew wealthy in silver while Westerners enjoyed their new valuables. The famous love affair between the English and their tea started here, for example. But because China was only importing silver, it enjoyed a steadily growing trade surplus while all of its European partners experienced a trade deficit.

A trade deficit is not by itself a terrible thing, but it led to a decline in the silver available to Europe after a few centuries. When the growing empires of Europe started to hold on to their remaining precious metals in order to mint coins, trade with China ground to a halt. This ended up hurting European consumers more than Chinese producers, because China was able to combat stagnation or inflation by importing small but consistent amounts of silver from Japan.

Thus, European colonies in Asia began to look for a market where the Chinese would import as much as they did silver. Finding nothing, their more creative minds decided to just invent one.

So, those aforementioned cities in India and Indonesia began to produce huge amounts of opium. If opium merchants could increase the market for it in China—essentially get the empire hooked on drugs—then they would finally have a cheaper, renewable export to trade for Chinese goods.

The only problem was getting China to accept the stuff. Opium being illegal in China was certainly a challenge, but they wouldn't let that stop them. Trade companies could circumvent the law, or better yet change it, if they could just get a foothold in China. But to do that, they would need to do away with the Canton System.

The Canton System & Fallout of the Flint Affair

Prior to 1757, Chinese trade policies had a protectionist bent inspired by Confucian ideals. If a market or foreigner in that market was seen as harmful to societal harmony and Chinese values, contact with them was limited. The Qing Dynasty also often worried about commercial threats to their power from the outside world. And while some were imaginary, others were very real.

As a result of these protectionist policies, each foreign trade vessel docked in a Chinese city was beholden to a local merchant called a Hong. The Hong took responsibility for its crew and cargo and required them to pay taxes for any trade deals. The Cohong, the organization each Hong belonged to, was the direct intermediary between Qing Dynasty officials and foreign traders.

The Cohong system gave the Chinese government a high level of control over trade in its own cities. This frustrated European crews who had to pay high tariffs to a Hong and do exactly what the strict trade laws stated. These restrictions only got worse after a merchant named James Flint decided to ignore the laws and repeated warnings from the Qing government.

James Flint was a British merchant who chafed under the trade restrictions in the southern city of Canton, where his EIC ship was forced to dock for the whole trading season of 1755. Eventually he grew sick of the slow and controlled business in Canton and wanted to find new business opportunities in other Chinese port cities. He broke Cohong regulations and sailed north to the city of Ningbo in Zhejiang province. Instead of finding better trade deals, James Flint made trade for all Europeans even worse.

In 1757, two years after the "Flint Affair," the Single-Port Commerce System was put in place by the Qianlong Emperor. It became better known outside of China as the Canton System, because the only port where foreign ships were allowed to trade was at the city of Canton. It was no coincidence that Canton was where Cohong control of trade was strongest.

European merchants would fight this system every step of the way, including James Flint himself. Flint unlawfully embarked from Canton yet again in 1759, this time to file a complaint in Tianjin. He spent three years in a prison on Macau for that stunt.

But while legitimate traders fought a protracted war of diplomacy with the government in Canton and China at large, opium smugglers just continued to do what they always did.

An order to halt the illegal trade came down from the governor of Canton himself in 1799, and once again it was met with little success.

With the turn of the century, came a boom in opium trading, a political atmosphere balanced on the razor-thin line between civility and conflict, and some of the strangest smuggling tactics yet.

Chapter Two

The Opium Trade from 1800-1838

Floating Warehouses

As long as they remained low-key and bribed the right officials, Chinese opium dealers could freely move throughout China in ways that a European trader couldn't. But the inside agents of the opium trade still relied on foreigners to supply them. So when it became too conspicuous for European opium traders to dock in Canton for those arrangements, they simply moved their business offshore.

Europeans, mostly British, bought large numbers of old Chinese ships in the beginning of the nineteenth century. They then sailed the ships just past the mouth of the Pearl River, and anchored them at sea in big groups that didn't go anywhere.

This flotilla of old junks became the new stopping point for European opium ships, which would unload their cargo for payment and then sail back to India or the islands of south east Asia. The anchored ships, acting like floating warehouses, would store huge amounts of opium over time. Chinese dealers would then sail out to the ships and purchase the opium in exchange for silver.

Meanwhile, the Qing authorities were unable to do anything about these storehouse ships once they discovered them, because the Chinese navy was built to fight river battles against pirates and other local threats, and didn't perform well on open ocean. They were forced to sit by and watch as the EIC and other trade companies distributed opium up and down the coast of China with impunity, immune to inspection or confiscation.

Americans got in on the opium trade in the early 1800s, offering cheap but low-quality opium imported from the Ottoman Empire in the west. The competition between different western nationalities drove the price of opium down, making it even more accessible to the lower classes of China.

This increased the national addiction to opium, which increased its demand, which made the market even bigger as more and more foreigners joined in. Opium started to be paid for with silver. The Europeans, who often smuggled opium on the side for their legitimate businesses, then used this silver to buy Chinese goods and turn even more of a profit back home.

This little detail had terrible significance, because it showed the moment where the opium smuggling scheme truly succeeded: not only had foreign merchants found a product other than silver to trade with the Chinese, but the Chinese were now giving up their own silver in exchange for it.

The Chinese trade surplus was being reversed, and the nation's fortunes along with it. Even the Cohong families were eventually corrupted and turned around on the issue, tacitly letting the drug trade expand in Canton while reaping bribes and taxes from it. And with civil war wreaking havoc in the background, taxes were only getting higher.

The White Lotus Rebellion

The rest of China was not staying still while Canton and the rest of the southeast coast was infiltrated by opium. Peasants were working hard in their fields, artisans were making their living in towns, provincial governors were collecting taxes from them, and religious revolutionaries were fomenting rebellion in the hills. Were it not for the growing foreign influence on the coast, this would have been business as usual in Qing China.

The White Lotus Movement was a secretive religious and political movement which existed since the Mongols conquered China and formed the Yuan Dynasty in the thirteenth century. The movement rebelled countless times over the centuries. The White Lotus was made up of Han Chinese, who now sought to overthrow the Qing Dynasty and usher in an era of salvation in which the Buddha would return.

The movement was the desperate hope of desperate peasants, taxed into poverty by the increasingly corrupt officials of the Chinese government.

Despite being peasants untrained in war, the White Lotus managed to score several surprise victories over Qing troops before being subdued. Proof that the Qing army was weak inspired more peasants to rebel. A renewed rebellion started in 1794, in the Daba Mountains, in response to high taxes. This revolt would drag on until 1804, putting a huge strain on China's manpower and treasury that could have been spent combating the opium crisis.

The White Lotus wasn't defeated until the Qing forced hundreds of peasant villages into bigger fortress cities, where they were trained to fight their countrymen in militias. But after the Lotus was gone, those same militias rebelled against the government for their mistreatment. The Qing had created another problem for themselves, at a time when they really didn't need it.

More manpower and resources bled into the countryside, while more opium crept in to the coast.

The Foreign Quarter

Increasing dependency on the opium trade and other European-dominated markets forced Canton and Macau to grant large concessions to foreigners at port. Thanks to the industrial revolution, changes in government trade policy, and the development of liberal economic theories by figures like Adam Smith, the EIC was joined by more independent traders in Canton. Though, it didn't lose its monopoly on trade with China yet. This greater competition increased the influence of Europeans on China further.

By 1820, European merchants were living in Canton year-round, and becoming quite established within the city. The Thirteen Factories district was the center of European activity, and it grew until its proper name was replaced by the more popular "Foreign Quarter."

A chamber of commerce was built in the district, and the small group of elite European merchants who influenced so much of the trade in Canton—including opium—began to rise to places of political power in the region.

Two of the most infamous Foreign Quarter residents were the Scotsmen William Jardine and James Matheson. The two shrewd businessmen met in Canton in 1820 and quickly became partners, both in legitimate business and in opium smuggling. They formed a consignment and shipping conglomerate named Jardine, Matheson & Co. in 1828.

As a testament to their success, this conglomerate still operates in Canton and Macau two hundred years later, now known as Jardine Matheson.

Jardine was a skilled political schemer, and he can be credited—or blamed—with subverting Chinese authorities to further the drug trade. With Matheson's support, Jardine petitioned the British government to force greater recognition and trade rights out of China.

An enormous victory was won for entrepreneurs and the opium trade in 1834, when British Parliament ended the EIC monopoly completely. This change let anyone with money join in on the game. It's no surprise that many of the reformers in Parliament at the time were getting financial kickbacks from Jardine and Matheson.

In the year 1787, the EIC had been sending about four thousand chests worth of opium to China, each chest weighing about one hundred and seventy pounds or seventy-seven kilograms. This totaled to about three hundred and forty tons of opium a year.

By 1838, Britain was selling over fourteen thousand tons of opium to China per year—that's more than a forty-fold increase.

To put that in perspective, the average chronic opium addict in China at the turn of the twentieth century would be smoking about eight grams of opium a day. Fourteen thousand tons would allow for almost four million three hundred and fifty thousand extreme addicts to get their fix every single day for an entire year.

Of course, not all of the opium was going to a few severe cases. Uncounted millions were suffering from addiction. Opium had surpassed silver in value and was now used for bartering, or as currency. People paid and collected taxes in opium, despite drug trafficking now being punishable by death thanks to another imperial decree. The situation had become a powder keg, and Qing officials scrambled to do something about it.

Diplomatic Blunders & Insults

For the past thirty-odd years, a diplomatic dance of death was underway. Britain had the largest piece of the opium pie in Canton by far, but neither side wanted to wage an all-out war to resolve the conflict.

Unsurprisingly, the adamant opposition between the two parties led to more than one diplomatic crisis. Most of them were caused by British persons breaking the etiquette or conduct expected of them by the Qing government.

Many times over the decades, European governments sent delegations to the court of the Qing Emperors in order to negotiate trade between their nations. The British first arrived in 1793, followed by the Dutch mission in 1794, and the Russians in 1805, with the British attempting a second mission in 1816. All of their proposals were rejected by the emperors of the time.

Both times that Britain sent a mission, first under Earl George Macartney, and then Earl William Amherst, highlighted incompatible worldviews, as well as a few cultural misunderstandings.

Both ambassadors—as well as other European dignitaries—wanted the rights to exclusive use of islands off the coast of China for harboring ships and building warehouses. Or they petitioned for their nation's freedom to trade in other Chinese cities besides Canton.

These requests would put one European nation ahead of the other, with respect to the relatively equal trading rights which China granted them. To break that balance would have caused a new rash of political fiascoes as every other power in the area tried to garner the same advantage, which would be more of a headache for China. Understandably, the Chinese emperors declined their offers.

On top of that, both British ambassadors refused to perform a deep bow of respect, commonly called a kowtow, for the Emperor, because it was seen as an act of subservience toward a foreign ruler.

Their missions did not fall through just because of a kowtow, contrary to popular opinion both then and now. But their refusal of standard Chinese courtly etiquette while making demands of that same court is symbolic of the strained, misunderstanding relationship between parties.

This, coupled with the continued spread of opium, led to the slowly deteriorating *status quo*, which made conflict almost inevitable. And conflict did finally occur.

After the end of the EIC monopoly on Chinese trade, another British delegation was sent to China in July 1834. Rather than requesting specific land rights or broader trade agreements, the mission led by one Lord William John Napier of the Royal Navy was more general.

Napier's mission was to obey all Chinese regulations, communicate directly with Qing government officials like the Viceroy of Canton and Guangxi provinces without any intermediaries, survey China's coastline, and superintend trade in contraband opium. If that mission statement looks like one big self-contradiction, that's because it was.

Napier was unable to follow all Chinese regulations, because a firmly-entrenched part of China's relations with Europeans was the use of messengers and go-betweens to allow communication between Qing authorities and any representatives. By breaking regulations and trying to circumvent these formalities, Napier also angered the official he was attempting to meet. This caused Napier to fail in two tasks at once.

The Viceroy refused an audience with Napier, frustrating the Lord's order to oversee trade in the region. For reasons known only to him, Napier then decided that military force was an appropriate answer.

In what would be known as the Napier Affair, the naval officer sent two frigates to bombard the Chinese forts at Whampoa on September 11th. The stalemate was cut short when Napier suddenly fell ill with typhus, and he retreated to Macau where he died exactly one month later.

The skirmish was indecisive, with light casualties and damage on both sides. But the real wounds were diplomatic. Napier left Anglo-Chinese relations worse than he'd found them, though not before seeding the idea among other colonial officials that Britain should also seize Hong Kong.

Amazingly, all-out war between Britain and China did not come to pass yet. Both nations needed the other on some level, and it would take the burning of more bridges to finally set war in motion.

Britain's trading dominance was weakened by the affair without a doubt, and all British merchants were forced to leave Canton for a period of time after the battle, sent to either Whampoa or Macau.

In that vacuum, Americans and other European nations who had maintained peaceful trade ties with China moved in to fill that gap. This didn't remove the British from their position of power in the opium trade in the long-run, but it diversified the fingers in China's pot.

Lin & Elliot Enter the Scene

In 1839, the Daoguang Emperor appointed a prominent scholar and official named Lin Zexu to the post of Imperial Commissioner. He was tasked with eradicating the opium trade by any means necessary.

He began with an open letter directed at the British, personally addressing Queen Victoria. The letter questioned the morals of the British government and pointed out its hypocrisy in dealing with the Chinese. For the opium trade was strictly forbidden in Great Britain, yet the crown seemed to turn a blind eye to the trade in Asia.

Lin Zexu wanted to remove the plausible deniability and the benefit of ignorance from the heads of state, while also reaffirming his own mission. He stated:

"Your Majesty has not before been thus officially notified, and you may plead ignorance of the severity of our laws, but I now give my assurance that we mean to cut this harmful drug forever."

We can never know how Queen Victoria might have replied to Lin's letter, because it appears she never received it. It may have been lost in transit, or perhaps it had been intercepted at some point.

Regardless, Commissioner Lin moved forward with his duty without a reply from the British crown. He issued yet another ban on the sale of opium in the empire and ordered that all supplies of it be turned over to the Qing government.

This time, however, the decree was followed by effective action. Beginning in the spring 1839, the Pearl River was closed to all ships, trapping European traders in Canton. The Foreign District and its warehouses were searched, and the stockpiles of opium found within were seized.

More impressively, Qing naval forces under Lin's command managed to board and capture British ships in the rivers and at sea despite their disadvantage against British vessels. Here, they also destroyed the smuggled shipments of opium.

The British colonial administration in East Asia, which by now had headquarters in Hong Kong, was not pleased by the seizure and destruction of British merchandise, even if it was illegal contraband. Charles Elliot, Superintendent of Trade in China, saw Commissioner Lin's actions as an attack. He ordered all remaining British ships carrying opium to flee from Chinese-controlled waters, and to prepare for battle in the event of the occurrence of hostility.

The game of political chicken was ramped up by Lin, who responded by surrounding and cutting off the supplies and communication of the Europeans still in Canton, effectively laying siege to the Foreign Quarter.

Uncharacteristically for a British trade official in this time and place, perhaps because of recent memory of the Napier Affair, Charles Elliot was the one who offered concessions in order to avoid the situation escalating further. With the promise that the British government would reimburse them for their losses, Elliot convinced the trapped dealers in Canton to hand all of their remaining opium stockpiles over to Lin.

They did so, and by the end of May that year the Chinese government had seized and destroyed two hundred sacks of opium and over twenty thousand chests of it, totaling to more than one thousand two hundred tons.

This is a paltry number in comparison to the number of tons that had been imported that same year, but it was a highly visible victory, and the image of Qing personnel burying millions of pounds of opium in the sand of Cantonese beaches sent a clear message to the world.

In addition, Lin's letter on morality to the Queen was unintentionally validated by Elliot's promise. If the British government did compensate those traders for their smuggled illegal substances, it meant that Britain implicitly supported the drug trade outside of its own borders.

Unfortunately, the British government was aware of this trap. No compensation for lost goods was ever actually given, lest a political firestorm be unleashed back home in Parliament.

Charles Elliot's risky attempt to de-escalate the situation ended up being for naught. The indignity Britain suffered at the hands of the Emperor's official meant that the English now had a *casus belli*—a justification for the declaration of war, if they were inclined. But for the time being, Britain held on to its grudge.

Commissioner Lin later reopened trade and allowed it to continue under altered rules and new conditions. The strictest rule was that no more opium was to be shipped in to China in any way, and that all parties involved in transactions were equally responsible.

Lin had discovered the corruption and complacency of the major Hong families in his investigation of trade policy up to that point in time. He had been especially shocked to find that in all of the years of opium being unambiguously illegal, not one recorded instance of a complaint being filed about smuggled opium could be found in the Cohong archives.

This would not continue under his watch. All foreign merchants, as well as Qing officials, were ordered to swear a binding oath not to deal in opium, under penalty of death.

Officially, Britain objected to this because it violated its idea of free trade. But individual British companies who did not engage in opium smuggling were more willing to make the agreement, supporting the new Chinese regulation while driving a deeper rift between the two governments.

Ironically, the people made most happy by the arrangement were black marketeers. The sudden loss of stockpiles and supply lines raised the price of opium, making it an even higher risk, higher reward product to smuggle in to China. The drug was able to trickle in thanks to some European ships being told of the opium ban before docking, which allowed them to drop their shipments off elsewhere.

Further hamstringing the policy change was Charles Elliot's unwillingness to enforce it. He had orders to stop smugglers, but at this point tensions were so high between Britain and China he feared any naval action by his ships, even against smugglers, could be construed as an attack.

Things may have had a chance to simmer down from a boil, had violence stopped. But before they could return to the former *status quo*, a different drug was introduced into the mix. The metaphorical powder keg of China had its fuse soaked in alcohol, and then lit.

Flashpoint at Kowloon

On July 7, 1839, a group of British sailors in ships owned by Jardine, Matheson & Co. landed in Kowloon, Hong Kong. They joined some of their colleagues from some other English and American crews in the area, and began to drink heavily.

The powerful rice wine they drank fueled a violent altercation between two of the sailors and a local villager named Lin Weixi. Lin was savagely beaten by the sailors and died the next day, leaving his hometown of Tsim Sha Tsui in an uproar.

Superintendent Charles Elliot, who was in charge of the men, was quick to pay for damages. He offered a reward of one hundred dollars and two hundred dollars to anyone who could provide evidence of who was responsible for the fight or the murder, respectively.

He paid one thousand five hundred dollars in compensation to the victim's family and one hundred dollars to the village, as well as a smaller sum of four hundred dollars in "protection money," to guarantee the family would not be extorted for their money by local officials.

But Commissioner Lin Zexu was on the case, and once again he was not satisfied with Elliot's methods—a subject of the Chinese Empire had been murdered on Chinese soil, and so Chinese law would be followed accordingly.

Unfortunately, Elliot also took issue with this, because it would require that he hand his men over to be executed by a foreign power.

The two men were at an impasse. Elliot refused to turn the guilty parties in, and instead held court aboard an English vessel and tried the sailors with himself as judge. He found five sailors guilty, and sentenced them to fines and hard labor upon return to Britain.

Due to Elliot's lack of proper jurisdiction, these sentences would all eventually be overturned back home. Lin Zexu declined the offer to send observers to offer "comments" on the proceedings, seeing the naval court and its ruling as an obstruction of justice and a violation of Chinese sovereignty.

In response, Commissioner Lin ordered a ban on the sale of food to British residents in Canton until those involved in the murder were turned over. War junks were deployed on the mouth of the Pearl River to blockade the port, and—false—

rumors circulated that the Qing had poisoned the fresh water sources used by foreign ships.

This blockade of all trade continued until the end of August, when on the 23rd an opium smuggler ship was attacked by the river pirates who so often plagued the Chinese government.

A rumor quickly spread among the British that the Chinese navy attacked the ship, and as a precaution Charles Elliot ordered all British ships to leave the coast of China by the next day.

Withdrawn from Canton and forced out of Macau, dozens of ships and thousands of people were stuck idling off the coast of China with dwindling supplies. On August 30th, the heavily armed frigate HMS *Volage* arrived off the coast to defend the ramshackle fleet from any Chinese aggression.

Elliot demanded that the embargo end. Five days later, without any word on the end of the ban, he sent an armed cutter and schooner to Kowloon with an ultimatum for the blockade ships stationed there: allow shipments of food to pass through to the British by three that afternoon, or be fired upon.

The ships' guns were readied. The Qing forces made no reply. The deadline came and passed. The first volley was fired at fifteen minutes to four.

The "Battle of Kowloon," one of the early skirmishes of the First Opium War, had begun.

Chapter Three

The First Opium War, 1839-1842

The Battle of Kowloon

The HMS *Volage* was one of four British vessels firing upon Chinese blockade junks off the coast of Hong Kong. Though they were outnumbered and outgunned by the newer British warships, three junks sailed out to meet the British and returned fire.

The Chinese attempted to close the gap between them so the British would not be able to use their guns to full effect. Three times, the Chinese tried to catch the British ships in netting used to board an enemy vessel. But each time failed because the British ships—a cutter, schooner, pinnace, and barge—were smaller and more maneuverable than bulky Qing naval junks.

A battery of cannons on the shore joined the battle within the first hour, but not even this extra firepower allowed the Chinese to leverage anything against the enemy. Hundreds of rounds were fired from every ship during that long, fierce skirmish.

The British ships were also much faster. They were able to break away from the battle when they ran out of ammunition, outrun the junks chasing after them, and then resupply with fresh shot to continue the fight.

The *Volage* went on past the other three ships to get reinforcements, so the three remaining British ships fended off the junks until nightfall. The return of the *Volage*, plus an EIC ship called the *Cambridge* finally forced the junks to retreat back to their positions from the start of the day, and the battle ended in a stalemate.

Elliot was encouraged by his fellow officers to destroy the junks and land in the bay to attack the cannons with their extra firepower the next day, but the Superintendent declined. British civilians were still starving at sea or in the Foreign Quarter, and he didn't want to destroy the villages he had been trying to trade with for food. And after the battle, the Chinese ships weren't eager to tussle with the British again either.

Thanks to the corrupt navy of Canton, the British nationals soon got their supplies. Opportunistic Qing sailors had already been in the business of turning a blind eye to the local opium trade and extorting the locals for bribes. Before the skirmish at Kowloon, their demands had been too high for the villagers to pay. But after getting intimidated by the British, the ships were willing to accept smaller bribes not to notice any illicit food trade.

A battle had been fought for a war that wasn't declared yet, and the trade embargo was broken despite still being in full effect. Commissioner Lin would have had quite a headache writing a report about all of this, had he not been lied to.

In addition to taking bribes, Qing navy officers were not above embellishing their own battle reports in order to earn commendations or promotions. With the head of the imperial government so far away in Peking, it was easy to lie about how well a battle outside of Hong Kong went. So, Commander Lai Enjue sent a false report to Commissioner Lin that he had held the blockade and sunk an expensive two-mast British ship, killing forty to fifty men during the battle.

In reality, no British sailors died at Kowloon. Only three were wounded, which was even less than the two killed and six wounded Chinese combatants in the battle. Lies like this would proliferate throughout the Opium War, causing the leaders of the Chinese military to severely overestimate its naval superiority while the British position grew stronger.

The Chinese even had a name for what would later turn out to be disingenuous, over-hyped stories of victory. Kowloon was the first of the "Six Smashing Blows" against the British navy, but the only things being smashed would be more Chinese forces as the war started in earnest.

Commissioner Lin Zexu, China's best hope for resolving the opium crisis, was undermined by his own allies and kept in the dark when he might have been the most useful.

The First Battle of Chuenpi

What followed was an armed standoff between nations through the rest of summer and into autumn of 1839. Almost all trade, other than illicit smuggling of opium or supplies between China and Britain, ended after the Cowloon skirmish.

The only exceptions to this were the British ships whose captains signed the bond decreed by Commissioner Lin months earlier: swear not to deal in opium, or be executed. Charles Elliot, as the *de facto* commander of British military and trade vessels in China, ordered all ships—legitimate or not—to refuse signing the bond. His word was respected by many, but not all.

In October, a British merchant ship sailed in to the Chinese blockade of Canton, but was permitted to enter. It was the *Thomas Coutts*, a ship carrying cotton from Bombay, and it just so happened that the owner of the ship was a Quaker.

Quakers were vocally opposed to the British opium trade, and refused to deal in the substance. The captain of the *Thomas Coutts* also saw Charles Elliot's ban on signing the bond as unlawful, so he signed it and got on with his business with the Chinese.

In response, Elliot ordered a *counter*-blockade to be made. The HMS *Volage* and *Hyacinth* were stationed one mile south of the Chuenpi cannon battery outside of Canton on October 27th, to prevent any other British ships from reaching Chinese ports. Illegal or not, the EIC would not allow free trade—specifically the opium trade—to be undermined further.

Both blockades held without any ships passing through until November 3rd, when one of Elliot's own ships challenged them. *The Royal Saxon* defied the blockade and sailed to meet with Chinese junks, prompting the *Volage* to fire a warning shot in front of the *Royal Saxon*'s bow.

Sixteen Qing warships under the command of Admiral Guan Tianpei saw the warning shot and sailed out to defend the *Royal Saxon*. Seeing the Chinese junks as attackers, Elliot gave in to pressure from his officers to attack the blockade again.

The *Hyacinth* and *Volage* gave chase, once again outmaneuvering the Chinese junks to avoid their fixed-cannon fire before retaliating with their own barrages. They broadsided the junks, first from starboard and then from port side.

One junk exploded when its magazine was hit, and another three sank. Fifteen Chinese sailors were killed, while only one injury and some light damage to both ships was recorded for the British. Both forces withdrew at the end of the day.

Once again, the Chinese navy reported that it had won a great victory, so the opportunity to learn anything from the defeat was lost. Commissioner Lin was left in the dark, while Superintendent Elliot scrambled to pull his ships away from Canton before a reprisal attack came.

The British ended their counter-blockade and retreated to the sea around Portuguese-occupied Macau, where Elliot sued for assistance from its governor. He refused, for fear of damaging his relations with the Chinese.

Soon after, the British were forced to leave Macau, and by January 14th of the following year, the Daoguang Emperor asked all merchants to stop their dealings with the British in China. The British were on their own.

Declaration of War

It may come as a surprise that the people of Britain did not necessarily want a drug war with China. Contrary to the acts of the government and its associated trading companies, the public at large was outraged at the international opium trade. Many wished to have it contained and regulated, or even stop the sale of the drug completely.

The public in Europe and America both paid close attention to the way the opium crackdown unfolded. Many continued to sympathize with the Chinese, but a growing number of common people were upset at the "rude" treatment of British diplomats, the protectionist trade policies of the Qing, and the attacks on British vessels.

British Parliament was under the control of the Whig party during this time, and Whig-affiliated press did everything it could to paint a picture of Chinese "despotism and cruelty."

On January 16, 1840, two days after the Daoguang Emperor issued his request that all foreigners refuse service to the British in and around China, Queen Victoria made her annual Address to the House of Lords on the so-called "China Question."

She voiced her concerns for the upheaval and damages to trade, and said she would continue to give her "most serious attention" to these matters that were a threat both to her subjects and the dignity of her crown. The Queen herself was unhappy, and that never bode well.

The China Question immediately became highly politicized. The Tories, the opposition party, attacked the

Whigs for mishandling the opium crisis, lacking foresight, and neglecting to empower Superintendent Elliot with the authority he needed to deal with China effectively.

By April of that year the Tories were almost wresting control of Parliament from the Whigs, lighting a fire under the dominant party to do something to secure its position. Foreign Secretary Palmerston came on to the scene.

Palmerston was an aggressive foreign secretary and a die-hard supporter of free trade, so he naturally became the leader of the pro-war faction in Parliament. The anti-war camp, composed of mostly Tories and Liberals, was led by William Ewart Gladstone, future Prime Minister.

Unfortunately for the anti-war faction, the Whigs had the backing of many influential merchants who were being harmed by the opium blockade. These included the dastardly Jardine and Matheson, naturally, and the former consulted with Palmerston on how to formulate and pass a declaration of war on China. Following this, Palmerston wrote a letter addressed to Prime Minister William Melbourne, also a Whig.

The matter of war was finally brought before the House of Commons on April 9th, where it was debated over for three long days. The coalition of Tories and Liberal party representatives stood strong against the motion to declare war at first, but arguments in favor of armed conflict were extensive.

First came the long-held belief that the destroyed opium counted as property deserving of compensation, rather than contraband. Then came the justification that a war would control the payment deficit between China and Britain, hearkening back to the reason why the opium trade in China took off—but ignoring the fact that the trade surpluses were already reversing.

The insult from China's expulsion of several diplomatic parties still festered like wounds to Britain's pride, and it was easy to stir up antagonism with that memory. Finally, the pro-war camp went so far as victim-blaming by claiming that the Chinese consumers of opium were the real driving force behind the trade, shifting the moral blame away from suppliers.

On April 12th, the final votes on the matter were counted. Two hundred and sixty-two voted against the declaration of war, two hundred and seventy-one in favor. A difference of only nine votes set the British Empire on the path toward its next bloody conquest.

One last motion to block the declaration was made in the House of Lords one month later on May 12th, but that too failed.

It took until July 27th for the House of Commons to ratify a budget of one hundred and seventy-three thousand four hundred and forty-two pounds—a little over six million American dollars today—for the war, which had already been going on for an entire year.

The Palmerston Letters

In addition to funding and official support from Britain, Superintendent Charles Elliot also received new orders. He received a pair of letters from Foreign Secretary Palmerston: one addressed to the Emperor of China, the other to himself. Elliot was instructed to set up a blockade on the Pearl River once more before forwarding the Emperor's letter to a Chinese official.

In the lengthy letter to the Daoguang Emperor, Palmerston offered the official declaration of a punitive expedition, a lengthy list of demands, as well as the British justification for actions against China. In his own words:

"These measures of hostility on the part of Great Britain against China are not only justified, but even rendered absolutely necessary, by the outrages which have been committed by the Chinese Authorities against British officers and Subjects, and these hostilities will not cease, until a satisfactory arrangement shall have been made by the Chinese Government."

Palmerston outlined the demands made to China in the letter addressed to Elliot as well. It was a long list, and a culmination of all the grievances Britain had built up toward China over the last century. Highlights from the list include:

- Demand respect due to royal British envoys from Chinese officials.
- Give the Superintendent of Trade the power to judge British subjects in China according to British law.
- Obtain compensation for destroyed British property—i.e., opium.
- Give Britain the most favored trading status with China among European powers.
- Exempt Britain from the Canton System, as well as open Canton, Amoy, Shanghai, Ningpo, and Formosa—modern Taiwan—to free trade with all foreigners.

- Capture a number of defensible islands along the Chinese coast to use as forts, merchant stops, or bargaining chips.

As for how to meet those objectives, Palmerston left it up to Elliot's discretion. He did state in his letter that a diplomatic solution was preferable. But he also expressed to Elliot how skeptical he was of the Chinese honoring any agreements they did negotiate, making it clear that Elliot's mission was to secure a military victory for Britain by attacking and blockading the islands and river mouths of China.

Mobilization

Elliot was put in control of naval forces and British interests, while marines and land forces were commanded by Commodore James Bremer and Major General Hugh Gough, respectively. Their counterparts in the Qing were Lin Zexu, Admiral Guan Tianpei, and General Yang Fang.

Thanks to the faulty reports of victory against the British in every naval skirmish from Chuenpi going all of the way back to the Napier Affair, Chinese forces severely underestimated their enemy in the beginning of the war. Few preparations were made for the arrival of the British armada.

Making matters worse, Qing land forces were pulled away from the coast and mobilized in the Chinese southwest. This was done in case a border dispute between the Sikh Empire and the Qing subject of Tibet turned into all-out war. The Sino-Sikh War would indeed break out in the following year, but it would be a short, fruitless conflict that did nothing but weaken both empires against British incursion.

Because of these handicaps, the Chinese army that would face the British would be thoroughly unprepared and undermanned. On paper, the Chinese had hundreds of warships and over two hundred thousand soldiers at their disposal.

But in reality their ships were often unarmed or in disrepair, and their regiment lists were padded out with fake names or filled at the last second with untrained and demoralized peasants. Despite their numerical advantage, the Chinese would be hard-pressed to resist the British expedition of twenty thousand men with fewer than forty ships.

Even when the Chinese were fighting at their full strength, they were still rarely a match for the British. This is because morale, training, and leadership notwithstanding, the technology of the Qing Dynasty was two hundred years behind the British Empire. British infantry was equipped with guns and equipment which were state of the art at the time, and the ships and artillery that backed them were some of the finest in the world.

Less than fifty percent of Qing infantry even carried firearms. They were more likely to be armed with swords, spears, or pole weapons like pikes. Their cavalry units still fought like it was 1200 CE, charging straight into enemy lines to try and break them. When the Qing did have guns, they were commonly muzzle-loading muskets that were heavier, slower, and shorter range than the rifles of the British.

British forces had difficulties of their own, but they were less severe. Their biggest challenge was actually reaching China, because ships and regiments had to be drawn from all across the British Empire. Forces from England, South Africa, India, and Australia had to rendezvous in Southeast Asia.

Storms and unseasonable weather also slowed deployment and damaged the hulls of their most valuable vessels, including two, seventy-four gun war ships. Lack of immunity to infectious tropical diseases also meant that many British soldiers would get sick and die during the war—hundreds more than those ever killed in battle.

Inroads to China

In June 1840, British forces landed in occupied Singapore. They captured the Chusan Islands and their trace center of Dinghai by early July, suffering almost nonexistent casualties while Chinese junks and garrison soldiers were destroyed or died in the dozens.

The armada then split the expedition in to two halves. One fleet traveled south to begin the Pearl River blockade. The other, led by Elliot, sailed north into the Yellow Sea with the goal of delivering one of Palmerston's letters to the Emperor.

Finding invaders almost at his doorstep and suffering to read the list of outrageous demands they made of him, the Emperor of Qing decided that something had to be done. China had not effectively dealt with its opium crisis up to that point, nor its rash of upstart Westerners. Someone was to blame for all of this. And as bad luck and political machinations would have it, that person was Commissioner Lin Zexu.

After a little less than two years in office, the man who had crusaded against the opium trade was being scapegoated for its proliferation. Lin Zexu, a senior official so famous for his moral uprightness and integrity that he was known by the nickname "Lin of Clear Skies," was seen as lax in his duties. He was dismissed from his position as Viceroy of Lingguang, and replaced by high-ranking Manchu official named Qishan. China's hopes started to diminish a little bit faster.

But for the moment, the addition of fresh blood to the Chinese war administration seemed to have a positive effect. Negotiations immediately started between the Qing and Britain. Qishan represented China and Elliot continued to represent Britain's interests. They met in the middle of 1840, eventually settling on the Pearl River to begin the long, arduous process of negotiation.

A tentative goal for the talks was that the British withdraw from the Yellow Sea, in return for the Chinese paying for the damages suffered by British merchants. The war didn't stop while talks were going on, of course.

One side's military advantage would translate directly into a better position to make demands from the other at the table of diplomacy. Britain continued to push against Chinese defenses as the second half of 1840 dragged on in to autumn and beyond.

The scales tipped farther in Britain's favor after a six hundred-strong British Indian infantry division arrived as reinforcements. The Indians were accompanied by a ship which the Chinese would come to dread. The HMS *Nemesis* was a steam-powered warship made almost entirely of iron, impervious to the guns or fire rafts of the Qing navy.

The *Nemesis* only possessed eight guns, but two of those were massive thirty-two-pound canons on pivots. Most importantly, the ship's draft—the part of the hull that is below water—was very shallow, allowing the *Nemesis* to navigate the river systems of China that other ships couldn't maneuver in. The *Nemesis* would live up to its namesake well in to the First Opium War, that the Chinese allegedly called it the Devil Ship.

Macau was isolated from the rest of China on August 19th, in the Battle of the Barrier, causing the Portuguese in the city to drive out Chinese administrators and open their ports to the British.

This effectively gave the British the perfect port to attack the rest of southern China from, while Portugal officially remained neutral. After securing Macau in the south and Chusan in the north, the British were free to push their Pearl River campaign.

Admiral Guan Tianpei was not sitting idle while China's outlying territories were snatched up. When the British armada first arrived in China, only three thousand men garrisoned the forts of Humen outside of the Pearl River. By the time the British came knocking, that garrison had swelled to ten thousand with over three hundred cannons.

The Second Battle of Chuenpi began on January 7, 1841, with the Chinese offering the stiffest resistance yet. But no British ships were destroyed, and only a few dozen men were wounded, compared to more than a dozen junks and hundreds of men killed or captured on the side of the Qing. The Chinese were forced upriver, securing the British blockade of the Pearl River and exposing Canton to attack.

The Convention of Chuenpi

The Chinese realized how grave a blow this was. Their navy was at a disadvantage, and with the British controlling the rivers, not even their numerical superiority in infantry could avail them. Viceroy Qishan realized how bad things could become if the British landed in Canton. So he restarted the peace talks which had been dragging on for half a year now, but this time he led with a more generous offer than before.

Qishan agreed to pay six million silver dollars in damages for the British opium destroyed while Lin Zexu was in office. He also promised Superintendent Elliot the return of British prisoners, and for control of Hong Kong to be given to Britain in exchange for an end of the occupation of Chusan.

The opium trade would not be outlined in any legal—or illegal—terms, but trade in general would be opened back up between China and Britain no later than February 1st.

It seemed as though the British plan to force such a favorable political resolution with the threat of overwhelming naval superiority had been a huge success. This practice would come to be known as Gunboat Diplomacy, and it would be used countless more times throughout modern history. Often, it would echo the original theme of European powers dominating a sovereign East Asian state. Only a decade later for example, Commodore Matthew Perry would use the same technique to force Japan to open its harbors to the world.

Both representatives signed the treaty, and a ceasefire began as copies of the agreement were sent to their respective leaders. The only issue is that neither the Daoguang Emperor nor Foreign Secretary Palmerston wanted anything to do with the Chuenpi convention. The Emperor refused to give up any

Qing territory which he had not personally signed off on, while Palmerston wanted many more concessions to be forced out of the Chinese, as his letters had outlined.

Both Qishan and Elliot were removed from their posts by their angered superiors, with Qishan narrowly escaping a death sentence for the blunder. But Elliot would not become aware of his replacement until July of that year, meaning that British actions in China wouldn't be damaged by a change of overseers the way the Qing administration was. The February deadline for the reopening of trade came and went, and hostilities picked right back up. Peace would not come easily.

Fighting Upriver

February saw two more battles along the Pearl River. The Battle of the Bogue from February 23-26, saw the British capturing more Chinese forts in the Humen Strait, known to the British as the Bogue.

It allowed for another incremental advance toward Canton, and played out the same as other battles had up to that point: the better-equipped British navy and highly disciplined infantry outmaneuvered the more numerous but demoralized and poorly outfitted Chinese forces, causing very lopsided casualties while only suffering a few injuries. The death of

Admiral Tianpei in battle threw the Chinese navy into further disarray.

It wasn't until the Battle of First Bar on February 27th, that the British finally suffered a single casualty, but that kill wasn't thanks to luck or prowess on the part of the Qing. An English sailor allegedly got the hammer of his musket caught on a ship strut while aboard the HMS *Modeste*. The musket misfired, shooting him in the head, but the British victory proceeded without issue. Even the *Cambridge*, an EIC ship bought and fitted for war by the Qing, couldn't stand a chance against its former fellows.

March 2nd saw the British capture the island of Whampoa, putting them within range to attack Canton itself. Both sides realized how pivotal the battle here would be, so both agreed to a three-day ceasefire to plan. The British fleet was reinforced by the soldiers who evacuated Chusan as part of the ill-fated Chuenpi Convention, and General Yang Tang had reinforced Canton with over thirty thousand men.

While the British reinforced their position at Whampoa, a small detachment of ships cleared out the remainder of the Chinese forts and gun installations that threatened their advance. The Broadway Expedition, as it came to be known, left Canton exposed and almost defenseless by water. By March 16th, the British had the power to attack Canton, but they couldn't decide if they wanted to go through with it.

Elliot considered opening peace talks again, now that the British had a much stronger position to make demands from thanks to gunboat diplomacy. But while Elliot dallied, the Chinese fortified Canton and prepared for the battle that they thought inevitable. Qing engineers built fortifications and obstacles out of earth and destroyed junks, and prepared as many ships as they could. The Qing also removed all tea and silk from Canton in order to cripple trade that might benefit the British.

Once again, something that could have ended the war early was snatched away by a single violent incident. On March 16th, a British ship flying a flag of truce was fired upon by one of the Cantonese forts, prompting the British to burn the fort down to the ground. This was enough to convince Elliot the Chinese meant to keep fighting, so any pretense of diplomacy went out the window. On March 18th, the British attacked Canton.

The Battles of Canton

The First Battle of Canton was over almost as quickly as it had begun. The Chinese garrison had to be spread out across the entire city and its nearby countryside to guard it, but the British only needed to strike one point hard enough to get a foothold. They did so by attacking the very first place where Europeans had set up shop in China in the beginning of the opium trade: The Thirteen Factories District.

The British took the foreign quarter with few casualties and headquartered themselves at the old British factory, where they added insult to injury by raising the Union Jack of the United Kingdom over the city. The British made a few advances on to high ground after that, but by March 20th, the battle was over.

Trade was reopened after the British negotiated with the Cohong families, who were as opportunistic as ever. Tea, silk, and most importantly opium flowed back in to Canton, now the tarnished jewel of southern China.

Another truce was declared, and while British forces remained in control of the heart of Canton, Elliot sent the majority of the navy back downriver as a gesture of goodwill. This truce held through March and into April, when the replacement for Viceroy Qishan arrived in Canton. Yishan, cousin of the Daoguang Emperor, decided to parley with the British, since conditions had grown even worse for China since Qishan was dismissed.

Yishan ultimately agreed to keep trade open between Canton and Europeans, but this wasn't a sign of weakness. While trade did mean that opium was continuing to pour into Canton, it was still a source of wealth for China. With all of the money flowing in from trade, Yishan immediately began to rebuild the scattered Qing army in secret. The truce of Canton was the perfect cover for a military buildup, especially with so many of the British ships sent south.

The Qing army around Canton was raised to fifty thousand men. Artillery was placed and hidden along the Pearl River. Soldiers were deployed to lie in wait for ambushes at Whampoa and the destination for the British fleet down in Bocca Tigris. Hundreds of fishing boats and other small craft were outfitted with matchlock guns, and even more rafts were built, tethered together, and then loaded with flammable materials to turn into a floating wall of fire at a moment's notice. Every last bit of desperate ingenuity the Qing military had, it used. The date was set. May 21st would be the night they retook Canton.

Unfortunately, the British got the memo ahead of time—literally.

In preparation for the Second Battle of Canton, the Daoguang Emperor circulated a missive for the Chinese army to read and boost their morale. It commanded Qing forces to "exterminate the rebels at all points," and described how this would only be the beginning of Chinese victory. They would push the British down out of the Pearl River, retake Hong Kong, and ultimately drive them out of all of China.

The missive was leaked to the citizens of Canton, including the British, at some point before the battle. This confirmed British suspicions already aroused by rumors of the Qing military buildup. When prominent Cohong families started to flee Canton in early May, the looming threat was all but confirmed. They just didn't know exactly when the axe was going to drop.

On May 20th, Yishan made a statement assuring the people of Canton that there was no chance the Chinese hosts surrounding Canton were going to result in any hostilities whatsoever. This had the opposite effect of inciting worry, and Superintendent Elliot ordered all British residents to evacuate the city by sundown the next day. He also recalled several battle ships to Canton. Later that night, the Pearl River was lit on fire.

The Qing coordinated an attack by land and river under the cover of darkness, bombarding the British ships outside of Canton while soldiers surged into the Thirteen Factories. The Chinese were successful in reclaiming the British Factory and the Foreign Quarter, but was unsuccessful in pinning down the rest of the British fleet before it could mobilize for a counterattack. The chain of fire rafts was ignited too close to Canton, and it caused the city's docks to catch fire.

Despite the haphazard execution, the Chinese regained control of Canton for four days while the British regrouped and met reinforcements from Hong Kong. They struck back hard on May 25th, capturing the factories and the artillery positions in the highlands around the city.

The Qing army was broke and fled in to the countryside under bombardment from land and sea, and the British followed to stamp them out.

What followed was a brief episode of guerrilla conflict that would have unexpected consequences throughout modern Chinese history. While the Qing army routed and ran away,

Chinese peasants angered by the presence of foreigners in Canton rose up to face them.

In what would come to be known as the Sanyuanli Incident, over twenty thousand Chinese villagers armed with spears and swords lured British infantry into the rain-soaked marshes north of Canton where their muskets were useless. There, they attacked the British in successive waves, managing to kill several British soldiers and Indian Sepoys.

The casualties suffered were fairly light, but the British were annoyed enough that they threatened to burn Canton to the ground if the attacks continued. The governor of Canton province was cowed into complying, and tried to dissuade the peasants. This only angered the people more and had the governor labeled as a traitor to the people of Canton.

The British quickly forgot about the incident at Sanyuanli, but it was immortalized in Chinese history as a sort of Alamo moment. The corrupt dynasty was too weak to defend its people from foreign barbarians, but the common people were able to rise up together and fight them with—little more—success. A century later when China was in the midst of first republican and then communist revolutions, the Sanyuanli Incident became powerful nationalist rhetoric.

Peasant heroism aside, the battle to retake Canton was a failure for the Chinese. The entire British force returned to the city and by May 30th the whole city was under their control. Chinese leaders were forced to capitulate, and agreed to a lopsided peace treaty later nicknamed the Ransom of Canton. Elliot signed the agreement, once again without the approval of his superiors. The British were paid a huge amount of money to leave Canton, which they did the next day in order to go and secure their new headquarters in Hong Kong.

Viceroy Yishan was left to write an official report for the Emperor. He decided to learn all of the wrong lessons from the administrations of Lin Zexu and Qishan, and instead of telling his cousin the truth, Yishan lied to the Emperor about what had happened. He claimed the defense of Canton had been a success, and that the British had thrown themselves at his mercy and begged for the peace treaty. Nowhere in his report did he mention the British fleet remained undefeated and ready to continue the war.

North to Amoy

The ceasefire continued in to July, as Qing commanders and British expedition leaders argued over what was to be done, or how. The Daoguang Emperor still wanted the goals of his Canton missive achieved, including reclaiming Hong Kong and driving the British out of China. Meanwhile, Superintendent Elliot wanted to end the conflict and reopen trade using their stronger position, while British military leaders such as Major General Gough wanted to press the attack.

The British stalemate was ended on July 29th, when Elliot was finally alerted to the fact that he had been removed from his post by Foreign Secretary Palmerston months ago. The news preceded his replacement, Henry Pottinger, who arrived in Hong Kong on August 10th.

Pottinger *did* want to negotiate terms with the Qing, but not for just the Pearl River. He wanted to give Britain a stake in all of China when the war was ended. So he sent away any Chinese diplomats who tried to speak with them, and made plans with the commanders to bring the fleet north and threaten the imperial capital of Peking—modern Beijing.

To do this, the British captured the city of Amoy on August 27th, by which point the city had been abandoned by its populace after word came of the British success up and down the Jiulong River leading to them. Palmerston had wanted Amoy to be another international trade city in China, so strict limits were put on how the army could behave in the city. Looting or destroying property was punishable by death.

Eventually, the British relocated to a nearby island so as to not damage the city during occupation. Unfortunately this left the city unguarded, and a frenzy of looting started as swarms of desperate peasants, Qing army deserters, and general outlaws flooded in. The Qing army returned and pacified the city before the beginning of September.

Naturally, this struggle to barely break even was reinterpreted by the governor of Amoy as a smashing victory in which five fictional British vessels had been sunk. The misinformation grew deeper.

Ningbo & How to Loot It

British forces captured Chusan for a second time on October 1st, after fear of China fortifying the island's defense outweighed British loyalty to the Treaty of Canton. With the harbor at Dinghai secure again, British forces were able to prepare for more strikes deep in to the interior of China. This led to the invasion of Ningbo along the Yong River on October 10th.

Yet another lopsided victory for the British led to a large amount of captured booty from the city. This prompted British command to decide how they should seize the spoils of war, since Britain was still justifying much of the war by saying that it was a fight to get Chinese reparations for British damages.

Superintendent Pottinger argued that a percentage of all looted property should be taken, while Major General Gough worried this would anger the Chinese populace too much to be worthwhile. Eventually, a ten percent tithe was decided on, and wealth started to bleed out of China even faster.

British aggression slowed to a halt for the 1841 winter, giving the Qing time to regroup and understand just what was happening. The Daoguang Emperor *finally* began to suspect that he was being lied to. He ordered fact-checking from an independent third party in the form of the governor of Guangxi province—which wasn't being invaded—and through these more realistic reports he learned of the duplicity of his governors and generals.

Viceroy Yishan was stripped of his office, and cities across China started to fortify themselves against a much larger threat than before. But it was too little, too late. British forces were too difficult to repel with the resources and tactics the Chinese had, and recapturing cities from them was effectively impossible.

This futility was made painfully clear when Yijing, another cousin of the Emperor, mounted a counterattack on Ningbo in March of 1842. Qing forces out numbered the British garrison by five-toone, but the British use of technology was once again too strong to compete with.

Chinese infantry was lured into the empty city streets, thinking they were abandoned, only to be cut down and slaughtered in the hundreds by hidden cannons, mines, and riflemen in killing fields. The survivors of the Qing army fled, and the British hunted them down until they captured the city of Cixi in March.

The general campaign against the central China coast and its rivers ended with the tragic siege of Chapu on May 18th. The garrison was taken by surprise by the British attack and bombardment, except for a group of three hundred Manchu bannermen who holed up in a temple at the port city's center. The Manchus fought with such determination that even Major General Gough was impressed, but eventually the temple was overrun, the city captured.

The Han Chinese population of the city was quick to negotiate a treaty with the British. The surviving Manchu civilians, however, were as resistant as their soldiers. They reportedly committed mass suicide rather than being taken prisoner. Almost one thousand five hundred men, women, and children died that day.

The Yangtze River Campaign

With so many major ports blockaded or directly under British control at this point, the British had most of their war objectives in order. All they had to do now was force the Qing government to capitulate. To do that, the Qing had to run out of armies to field. Even if they were so poorly equipped and prepared, Chinese armies were still too big to ignore.

To break the war machine, the British decided to cripple the government's revenue. With no money to pay them, Qing soldiers would be even less willing to fight.

In May and June of 1842, a British fleet of twenty-five ships and ten thousand men sailed up the Yangtze, one of the last major river systems not already under their control. The fleet ignored towns and forts on the river for once. Instead, they targeted the tax collector barges of the Emperor himself.

The barges were captured and their masses of wealth were seized, crippling China's tax revenue for that year.

After emptying China's treasury, the fleet attacked and captured the mouth of the Huangpu River and the towns of Wusong and Baoshan. Shanghai fell next, looted in a chaotic three-way between Qing deserters, British soldiers, and Chinese civilians.

These victories exposed the major city of Nanjing to attack. Nanjing, known as Nanking to the British, was one of the oldest and most important cities in China. If it fell to foreigners, the blow to China and the Qing Dynasty could be fatal.

Unfortunately for Chinese strategists, an attack on the imperial capital of Peking would be just as deadly. And ever since they had taken cities in the area of Amoy, British forces seemed ready to do just that. Attention had to be divided between the two cities, and their defenses suffered as a result. Less than sixty thousand Manchu and Han soldiers stood between Nanjing and the British fleet—and considering the track record the Daoguang Emperor had recently been made aware of, that just wouldn't be good enough to win the battle.

So the Emperor devised a plan in secret to reach out to the British and sign a short-term treaty. As with Canton, the British would be paid a huge sum of money to leave the Yangtze river. This wouldn't have ended the war, but it would have given China a reprieve, and time to pull itself back together. But the plan was not acted on in time, and on July 14th, British ships sailed up the Yangtze from Shanghai.

Along the way to Nanjing the British stopped at the city of Zhenjiang, or Chinkiang as they called it. Zhenjiang was of huge strategic importance because it was located at the meeting of the Yangtze River and the Grand Canal, a huge artificial river that kept half a dozen Chinese provinces fed and functioning.

Zhenjiang had already suffered from the British advance, because its soldiers and cannons were the ones killed or captured at Wusong weeks earlier. Paranoia and disorganization were rampant among the city officials, and as many as one hundred "traitors" were executed in the ensuing breakdown of public order even before the British arrived on July 14th. The few river forts still protecting the city were blown to pieces by British artillery, and then the real battle began.

The outnumbered Qing garrison started the battle by fleeing from the city, leaving it looking empty and deserted like Amoy had been. But after disembarking and entering the city, British infantry was caught by surprise. Thousands of soldiers hiding in wait poured out onto the streets. They surrounded the British, and a bloody close-quarters battle raged across the city.

The British suffered almost forty casualties—the most British killed in a single battle in all of the war—but they were victorious. Chinese losses were staggering as usual. Those numbers became even worse when Manchu civilians, fearing what the British would do to them, committed mass suicide just like they did during the siege of Chapu.

One last atrocity would take place before the war's end. This one was committed against the British, instead of by them. On August 10th, after months of detainment and mistreatment, the crews of the captured British ships *Nerbudda* and *Ann* were executed. The ships had run aground on reefs off the coast of Taiwan during September of 1841 and March of 1842, respectively.

Their surviving crew members were held in captivity until news of the defeat at Zhejiang reached the Daoguang Emperor, and he gave the order to have them killed in reprisal. Over two hundred prisoners of war—mostly Indian conscripts—were executed.

The Nerbudda Incident was a last thumb in the eye of Britain before its inevitable victory, and a symbol of how ugly the First Opium War had become. Cruelty was met with more cruelty, just as greed had begotten more greed when the opium market first grew.

The Treaty of Nanking

The defeats, blunders, and outright tragedies of the war had finally broken the resolve of the Chinese to continue fighting. The British sailed toward Nanjing at the beginning of August, and were in position to lay siege to the city by the 11th. No order came down from the Daoguang Emperor to allow for negotiations, but the city officials did so anyway. Trade and reparations weren't worth this much death and disgrace.

On August 14th, a Chinese delegation led by the statesman Qiying left Nanjing to meet with British commanders aboard the HMS *Corwallis*. Negotiations lasted for weeks as the British made their demands and insisted that the Emperor personally accept the treaty. Many of

Palmerston's original demands were revisited during the negotiations, and a surprising number of them would be met.

The Emperor finally gave his diplomats the authority to sign a peace treaty in his name on August 21st, and on the 29th, Qiying and others signed an agreement alongside Superintendent Pottinger. The treaty was ratified by the Emperor on October 27th, and by Queen Victoria on December 28, 1842.

June 26, 1843, marked the formal start of the treaty, though the war had effectively been over for months.

The Treaty of Nanking was divided in to thirteen articles. The first ended the war, and the rest mostly focused on a new trade agreement between China and Britain. To a lesser extent, this affected Chinese relationships with other European powers.

Free and unrestricted trade was the name of the game. The Cohong and Canton Systems were destroyed, and four extra cities—Fuzhou, Shanghai, Amoy, and Ningpo—became so-called "treaty ports." It was in these cities that British subjects were able to do business with any whom they pleased, while answering only to British law. Other Europeans and Americans could do much the same, making Chinese markets a playground in which Westerners could compete as they pleased.

The lucrative opium trade would not be legal *per se*, but it would be untouchable thanks to this treaty. The trade tariff was also set by Britain, rather than China. In addition, twenty-one million silver dollars would be paid to Britain by China for damages over the next three years—plus interest. On top of that, the island of Hong Kong was ceded to the British Empire as a trade outpost indefinitely.

In return for all of this, Britain promised not to interfere with Chinese trade further inland, and withdrew all of its forces from conquered areas like Nanjing and the Great Canal. Other areas would only be free of British troops after reparations were paid in full years later.

No other concessions were given to the Chinese who had suffered almost twenty thousand deaths and millions of dollars in damages over the course of the war.

It is not hard to understand why, in later years, the Chinese would see the Treaty of Nanking as the first of the terrible Unequal Treaties, or that the First Opium War marked the beginning of a Century of Humiliation.

And it was just the beginning.

Chapter Four

The Interwar Period, 1842-1856

Anti-Manchuism

There were dozens of dynasties over the course of Chinese history before the Qing. Some were small and short-lived, and others had been powerful and lasted for centuries. But all of them eventually came to an end, to be replaced by a new upstart dynasty in a time of weakness. This cycle was so important in classical Chinese history that it was given a religious explanation and justification known as the Mandate of Heaven.

The Mandate of Heaven was essentially the divine seal of approval that every emperor of China claimed to have. It meant that the emperor and his dynasty were just and righteous, and this would be reflected in the success and prosperity of China. But if the dynasty and its rulers became corrupt, the Mandate of Heaven would be taken from them, and tragedies and natural disasters would befall all of China until a new authority proved itself.

It wasn't hard for a student of Chinese history to see that every dynasty eventually lost its favored status. And now that it looked like the Qing Dynasty had just gone through the worst beating of its existence, and foreign barbarians were running rampant through China with no one to stop them, many people started to suspect that the Qing was also corrupt and unfit to rule. That the number of Chinese subjects addicted to opium would *double* after the First Opium War only made things worse.

It didn't help that the Manchu elites of the dynasty, despite sharing some parts of Chinese culture, were also seen as unwelcome foreigners by many ethnic Chinese. There had been small uprisings against Manchu rule for years, including the White Lotus Movement that came before the First Opium War. But those rebellions had always been small compared to the millions of Chinese subjects who remained loyal to the empire. The resentment had always been on the fringes.

But now, anti-Manchu and anti-Qing sentiments were front-and-center. More and more rebellions broke out in the decade following the First Opium War, as more groups finally disconnected from the Qing. Many of these rebellions were by ethnic or religious minorities like the Muslim Hui people. Others involved Han Chinese who explicitly wanted to overthrow the Qing, or even reinstate the Ming Dynasty.

The rebellions sprouted up so frequently now that the devastated Qing military couldn't squash them all. The Sino-Sikh War was still raging far to the west, sapping resources that could have been spent elsewhere.

To make matters worse, there would be a regime change in the middle of it all. The Daoguang Emperor died in 1850, at sixty-seven, and was succeeded by his eldest son, Yizhu.

Yizhu took the title of Xianfeng Emperor at only nineteen. He was noted as a good administrator—at least in comparison to his brothers—but the young emperor lacked the experience to deal with all of the threats China was facing inside and out.

All of this is to explain how an upcoming conflict could be so destructive despite its most unlikely of origins. China had once again become the perfect powder keg for a disaster, and the person to light the fuse would be a failed civil servant with a god complex.

The Taiping Rebellion

Hong Xiuquan was a Hakka man born in 1814, in a poor mountain village in Canton province. He had an interest in scholarship at a young age, and his family bankrupted itself to get him an education and allow him a chance to take the Chinese civil service exams that would allow a man of almost any social background to become a government bureaucrat. This was virtually the only form of social mobility a man had access to in traditional Chinese society, besides a gruesome military career.

Hong failed the civil service exams three times in a row throughout his young adulthood. This is unsurprising considering that the exams had a less than one percent pass rate, but it crushed Hong all the same. He had a nervous breakdown and began to have feverish, prophetic dreams while recovering.

He actually thought he was the son of the Chinese creator god, Shangdi, and that his divine father and brother had given him the mission to destroy all of the Manchu "demons" infesting China. Later, after learning about Christianity from some European missionaries who'd been allowed to preach in China by the Treaty of Nanking, Hong mixed the two religions together.

Hong proclaimed himself the brother of Jesus Christ in 1843. He gathered followers, who helped him codify his belief system into the God Worshiping Society.

The Society offered starving and overtaxed Chinese peasants protection, and a promise of a new society with radical social reforms. Land would be socialized, all people within a village would be treated as members of a single family in order to halt blood feuds, corrupt Qing authorities would be undermined, foreigners would be cast out, and most importantly, things such as slavery, foot-binding, and opium would be made completely illegal.

Communities converted *en masse* after Hong and his followers successfully defeated bandits and pirates who'd been plaguing the wilderness around Canton for decades. By 1850, Hong had tens of thousands of fanatical followers.

This unorthodox religious movement became a rebellion after Qing officials launched a campaign of religious persecution against the trouble-making God Worshiping Society in Canton.

Guerrilla war quickly escalated into all-out war as hundreds of thousands of civilians, mercenaries, reformed bandits, and other irregulars joined the Society's fight against weakened Qing forces. Thanks to European arms merchants active in Canton, the rebels soon had access to better guns than the proper armies they were fighting against.

On January 11, 1851, Hong Xiuquan declared himself Heavenly King of the Taiping Heavenly Kingdom, making himself a direct competitor with the Qing Dynasty for sovereignty of China. The new kingdom consolidated its borders and then pushed into the rest of China.

The resulting fourteen year-long Taiping Rebellion deserves a book of its own to do justice to the social upheaval and harm it caused to China. But for a taste of its destruction, consider how bad the First Opium War had been. For all its economic devastation, the war "only" killed up to twenty thousand people. The Taiping Rebellion meanwhile caused the deaths of between twenty and thirty *million* people.

Entire provinces were emptied, cities were burned to the ground, and the ailing Qing Dynasty became even more feeble. At one point in the war, China even had to rely upon French and British forces who came to protect trade cities—

and their huge stores of opium—from the Taipings and other rebels looking to destroy them.

The war would eventually end after the Heavenly Kingdom was divided by civil war and its rulers became increasingly secretive and corrupt, but the damage was done. The Taiping Rebellion was—and still is—the bloodiest civil war in history, and it weakened China when the nation needed to be strengthening itself to face European imperialism and growing rates of opium addiction within its borders.

European Resentment

Europeans, meanwhile, were getting sick of having to support the Qing Dynasty against so many rebellions. As if the terms of the Treaty of Nanking had not been good enough, British colonial forces began to think that they were not getting enough out of China to make their effort worthwhile.

In addition to the British Treaty of Nanking in 1842, the French and Americans settled their own treaties with China at Huangpu and Wangxia, respectively. Other Europeans got their own trade deals over time, adding to the list of "Unequal Treaties." These all gave similar concessions to the Westerners in question, and also allowed for future renegotiation of the treaties.

The economic devastation of the 1840s and 1850s impacted trade with foreigners, causing each nation to try ratifying more and more intrusive deals with China, which would give them better control over the markets they were involved in—free trade only needed to be free for the winners, it seemed.

Chinese citizens were painfully aware of this inequality, and their resentment boiled over in to violent protests once in a while. Mostly aimed at the British merchants or their goods in and around Canton, these assaults usually weren't lethal, but they were highly visible and extremely disruptive of relations between Britain and China. Several of the thirteen factories were even destroyed in fires during these riots.

Eventually the governor of British Hong Kong felt a need to put an end to this, while also saving face for his nation. He demanded justice and reparations from Qiying, the diplomatic statesman who was now the new Viceroy. Qiying dragged his feet appeasing the British, so a military fleet eventually set sail for Canton in 1847.

Fortunately the Expedition to Canton caused no loss of life. The expedition of six ships and about one thousand men made stops at over a dozen surviving river forts on the way toward Canton. Each fort surrendered and its canons were spiked by the British. Spiking was the act of hammering a metal spike into the vent of a muzzle-loading gun, making it impossible to fire until the spike is painstakingly removed.

Over eight hundred guns were disabled like this, humiliating the Qing military. When the British threatened to attack Canton, Qiying capitulated and ordered punishments for the attacks on British nationals. Qiying was booted from his position as Viceroy for this poor handling, though he remained politically active elsewhere.

The Arrow Incident

While China's *de facto* imperial masters penetrated deeper into Chinese affairs, the Qing government resisted in any way that it could. Opium was pouring into the coast of China, but it was still illegal according to Chinese law. And while Lin Zexu was long-gone, other Imperial Commissioners had been fighting as hard against the trade in the meantime. One such official was Ye Mingchen.

He became governor of Canton after Qiying's dismissal, and while there he aggressively rooted out opium in the city. He also refused British entry in to the city, claiming they had no right to reside there.

He was technically correct, because on top of being extremely lopsided, the Treaty of Nanking actually read very differently in Chinese vs English, and in Chinese the British could not live indefinitely in Canton. So, Ye was able to honor the treaty while still doing his job and doing everything he could to undermine the British.

For his steadfastness, Ye was made the new Viceroy and Commissioner, and he used both those offices to attack opium harder. Unfortunately, while Ye was willing to work in the grey areas of the Unequal Treaties, British agents were willing to surpass that and go straight in to armed conflict. This back-and-forth continued for a few years, with Ye resisting on an issue for as long as he could until the threat of British guns made him change his mind.

Eventually this came to a head. In October 1856, a ship suspected of smuggling opium or anti-Qing rebels was seized under Ye's orders. It was Chinese-owned and crewed by Chinese, but it was registered under the name *Arrow* in Hong Kong, which meant that it arguably came under the jurisdiction and protection of the British. Hong Kong consul Harry Parkes demanded the *Arrow*'s release and compensation from Viceroy Ye.

Ye freed most of the crew members, but also kept several and did not release the ship or meet any of Parkes' other demands. Ye believed he was in the right, and would not bend to the consul. It turns out he was in the right, because the *Arrow*'s registration had expired some time before the incident, meaning that Hong Kong had no right or jurisdiction over it.

Parkes knew this, but pushed for compensation anyway. He even allowed others to believe the false rumor that the *Arrow* had been flying a British flag when it was captured.

He *wanted* to give the British an excuse to start another armed conflict with China.

He *wanted* to cause what would become the Second Opium War.

Chapter Five

The Second Opium War, 1856-1860

British Escalation

A British fleet reached the Pearl River from Hong Kong on November 23rd. It easily destroyed four river forts on its way to Canton, and on the 25th issued the ultimatum that Viceroy Ye allow the British back in to the city or it would be bombarded.

Ye refused, even as British guns were aimed at his own home in Canton. Starting the next day, the British fired one cannon at the city every ten minutes. In reply, Ye declared a bounty on every British head brought before him.

This slow, torturous bombardment continued for the next two-and-a-half months. The city was locked down, trapped in between British ambitions, and Ye's resilience—an unstoppable force and an immovable object. The siege was broken up by infantry assaults, reprisals, one-sided naval engagements, and failed peace talks. Sensing they were getting nowhere, the British finally returned to Hong Kong on January 5, 1857, to reconsider their strategy.

As with the First Opium War, Parliament had to fight its own battle over whether or not to declare a formal war on China, even as hostilities continued on the ground. The government coalition lost an initial vote on the *Arrow* Incident on March 3rd, but a general election in April gave them the majority in Parliament needed to make a pro-war decision.

An alleged Chinese assassination attempt on the governor of British Hong Kong and his family by arsenic poisoning added fuel to the fire on the debate floor, and ultimately helped turn things in favor of war. Lord Palmerston, former Foreign Secretary, also became Prime Minister.

They also made a resolution to request alliances from the United States and the Russian Empire, though this would be unsuccessful and both nations stayed neutral. Russia would remain completely uninvolved with the war, while the US navy fought a minor skirmish with China along the Pearl River before signing a treaty of nonaggression.

Later on in the course of the war, American ships would break the treaty and give secret aid to the British navy anyway. China, meanwhile, remained completely without allies. Japan, one of its only other Asian trading partners, wanted no part.

By May the Great Indian Rebellion of 1857, also known as the Sepoy Mutiny, was in full swing. The British government saw the conflict in India as more important, so forces en route to China were diverted to India. Britain dragging its feet to enter the war might have given China precious time to organize a defense, had they not entered conflict with another major European player: The Second French Empire.

France Wades In

During and after the destruction of the religious Taiping Rebellion, European missionaries and their Chinese converts were barred from many provinces in southern China. The government was suspicious of their intentions, and corrupt government officials were happy to extort them.

This was the fate of the French Catholic priest Auguste Chapdelaine, who refused to pay a bribe after he and a group of Chinese Catholics were arrested in Guanxi province in 1856. Father Auguste was accused of stirring up a religious rebellion by a local mandarin.

In response, he was savagely beaten and imprisoned on February 29th, where he died before his corpse was decapitated and his head was hung from a tree.

Auguste's death, as with any religiously motivated murder, was deeply unfortunate. But France had suffered through several such "martyrs" in the past without it severely damaging the relationship between France and China. But now that it seemed like Britain was going to surpass them in Asian colonial power, France used Auguste's murder to engineer their very own *Arrow* Incident. He would be the official cause for any opportunistic French involvement in the coming war.

Diplomatic messages were sent back and forth, and eventually the official who sentenced Aguste to death was demoted. But by the time the British were mobilizing for war, France's official stance was neutrality with "sympathy" for Britain. This sympathy turned into explicit military aid in

1857, and suddenly China was at war with two European giants.

Another Battle of Canton

Ye Mingchen refused an ultimatum sent to him by the British in early December 1857, demanding the reopening of Canton to foreigners, as well as expensive reparations for British costs and damages.

He did not even accept a promise that a ceasefire would be established if he agreed quickly, and that British and French forces would pull back until a new treaty was formulated. According to him, the British had already voided the Treaty of Nanking with their actions, and he did not have the authority to make a new treaty because only the Emperor could declare one.

The deadline for the ultimatum came and passed, and Ye stood his ground. Meanwhile British infantry under James Bruce, Lord of Elgin joined forces with a French army led by Jean-Baptiste-Louis Gros, supported by British Admiral Michael Seymour in late December. On the 28th, the combined Anglo-French force began an assault on Canton.

They intended to finally put an end to the nuisance Ye Mingchen had been to European interests in the province. The city was undermanned, as Ye was unwilling to spare the soldiers needed to fight the rebels inland. The time was right.

Once again, the suffering city of Canton was under siege. After a full day of bombardment, over five thousand Anglo-French soldiers landed and began to knock out the forts surrounding the city. The Chinese garrison believed that the European alliance would not move on to the city until after they had secured all of these forts, as they had done in the past.

But they were caught off guard on the morning of the 29th, when hundreds of French soldiers scaled the city walls directly. Their advance into the city was so fast that they actually ran in to their own artillery shells at one point.

While the French stormed the walls, the British continued the assault from the ground and eventually broke through one of the city's eastern gates close to the former Foreign Quarter. The defenders of the city were flanked and pinned, and the battle was quickly won by the allies.

A city of over one million people was captured by a force of less than six thousand. European casualties were as light as ever, with only eleven dead and a little over one hundred wounded. Hundreds of Chinese soldiers and civilians died from the bombing and assaults, as well as a fire that started in the city.

The operation didn't end with the city's capture, though. British soldiers searched through the streets of Canton, ordered by consul Parkes to hunt down Ye Mingchen and capture him. The viceroy was found soon after the battle, caught while trying to escape by scaling the wall of the bureaucratic residence he lived in.

Parkes, not the most graceful winner, enjoyed humiliating the uncooperative viceroy. Instead of being given the respect and treatment afforded to a person of Ye's rank, Parkes ordered him to be taken as another prisoner of war. He was shipped off to a British fort in Calcutta, India, where he would die a year later.

It is believed he starved himself to death, rather than let the British keep him as their prisoner. Yet another viceroy and imperial commissioner tried and failed to stem the tide of opium and European influence.

Capitulation at Taku & the Treaties of Tianjin

The war dragged on sluggishly after Canton was captured and occupied by the alliance. Europeans waited unsuccessfully for the Xianfeng Emperor to accept offers for peace talks with only minor skirmishes between the two sides, until May of 1858. The allies finally decided to force the issue by starting an offensive on the Hai River, which was the only waterway leading directly to the imperial capital of Peking.

The Hai was defended by a series of river forts known as the Taku Forts, and they were the biggest obstacles between the Europeans and the emperor himself. The combined armies made quick work of the Qing defenders yet again, conquering the second-to-last line of defense offered by the Taku Forts with light casualties on May 20th. The message was finally sent that the Europeans would not stop until the Emperor's doorstep. The Xianfeng Emperor authorized a group of diplomats to begin negotiating with the alliance on May 29th.

The emperor's two head representatives, Guiliang and Huashana, were not well-received at the Europeans' camp in Tianjin, then known as Tientsin. The allies had wanted someone of higher rank and treaty-signing authority to meet them face-to-face, specifically saying that they wanted someone like the former commissioner Qiying, who helped develop the Treaty of Nanking after the First Opium War.

Guiliang and Huashana were also less experienced than Qiying, and the Qing government started to worry that the peace process would go poorly if they were not guided. So Qiying was sent to Tianjin on June 2nd, where he would be prepared to use his expertise to advise the Chinese delegation, and to offer greater concessions to the Europeans—as long as they served China's interests and were within reason—when the situation required it.

But the Europeans had prepared for Qiying. When Qiying arrived on June 6th, he was barred from meeting the British or French representatives. The neutral American and Russian delegations received him, but they were not the nations whom China had the most at stake with.

The French and British also kept Qiying from meeting with Guiliang and Huashana so that they could take advantage of the less experienced negotiators. It wasn't until June 11th that Qiying was allowed to have an audience with his fellows and the British diplomatic mission.

Of course, the British were ready for that, too. The English interpreters Thomas Francis Wade and H.N. Lay demanded that the three Chinese officials agree to the British terms of peace wholesale, with no concessions made to China. When Qiying refused to allow it, the interpreters pulled out a series of documents, which had been looted from Ye Mingchen's home the previous year.

They were papers that contained an unflattering portrayal of westerners, and described how to deal with them in politics. These papers were written by Qiying himself, shortly after being forced to sign the first Unequal Treaties in the 1840s.

The British used sections from these decade-old angry notes to paint Qiying as a hateful anti-western influence who would only ruin the peace talks. Worse still, Guiliang and Huashana believed that Qiying had been sent to spy on them as much as assist them.

The duo were quick to throw Qiying to the wolves by sending word to Peking that his presence was hurting negotiations. The Xianfeng Emperor ordered Qiying to remain at Tianjin and serve China.

Stuck between a rock and a hard place, Qiying signed the British agreement and then fled Tianjin on June 12, 1858. Qiying was arrested and charged with defying orders and leaving his post, and then when a report of exactly what the

Treaty of Tianjin did, he was blamed for having participated in it.

He was sentenced to death for his almost inescapable disobedience, and committed ritual suicide on June 29th. His death did nothing to change the treaty, though.

The Treaty of Tianjin was actually a set of four treaties, one for each of the western powers who either declared war on China, or promised peace and neutrality only to side with the aggressors when it was safe and convenient to do so. Each treaty was similar in terms of what China was forced to give to all members of the alliance, with major clauses being:

- Conquered Chinese territory such as the Taku Forts would be returned to China.
- Russia was allowed to become another major player in Chinese trade. It shared the right to trade at all treaty ports along the coast.
- Seven more treaty ports were added to the list created by the Treaty of Nanjing, including Nanjing itself.
- China was forbidden from allowing monopolies to exist in its own domestic trade. Nothing was written to prevent Europeans from doing the same.

- American, British, French, and Russian subjects were given stronger extraterritoriality, and were permitted to travel anywhere in China.
- The preaching of Christianity by European missions was protected by law.
- European diplomatic legations—one step down from embassies—were allowed within the imperial capital of Peking.
- Six million silver dollars in damages were to be paid to Britain and France for the war.

After reading the contents of these unequal treaties and imprisoning Qiying, the Xianfeng Emperor began to regret accepting the offer to negotiate. The Qing court, which had initially supported Qiying and the peace process, was insulted by the treaty and became very hawkish.

The emperor refused to ratify the treaty, which technically meant that hostilities were not over yet. In late June, after being convinced by his court to continue the fight, he ordered one of his generals to prepare for more European attacks.

Return to Hostilities & the Second Battle of Taku Forts

Sengge Rinchen, an ethnic Mongol, reclaimed the Taku Forts and reinforced them to protect the Hai River, and therefore block European access to Peking. The Europeans knew the treaty wasn't accepted by the emperor yet, and saw this move as aggressive.

The following year they sent a force of about one thousand men and fifteen ships to drive off the Qing army of four thousand and a few dozen cannons scattered across six different river forts. They arrived on June 24, 1859, expecting another crushing victory like the ones that defined their track record for the past one-and-a-half wars.

What they got instead was the only major Chinese victory of the Opium Wars.

The Anglo-French force attacked just as low tide was hitting the river during a very muddy time of the year in eastern China. The ships sailed up to the forts to try and take them by land while bombarding them from the water, but got mired in mud and trapped before they got into range to land, or position to use their fixed guns.

Meanwhile Sengge Rinchen's men had a clear vantage point from up in their forts. Even with the shorter range and inferior design of Qing cannons, they were able to fire at the attackers like fish in a barrel.

The river stayed a muddy killing field for two days. At that point the British and French were able to retreat, but only with the covering fire of an American steamship whose captain broke the nonaggression pact between China and the United States.

The captain's justification was apparently racial in some way, declaring that "blood is thicker than water," and popularizing the expression for generations to come.

Between the three attacking parties, almost one hundred men were killed, over three hundred and fifty wounded, and seven gunboats damaged, destroyed, or abandoned and left grounded.

The Qing army finally got some small amount of revenge on the foreigners, and when news of the first verified victory reached Peking, Chinese morale and resistance soared. Back home the defeat was an embarrassment for Britain, and the empire took a blow to its pride and international prestige.

China was allowed to reinforce its position while the alliance retreated to lick its wounds. Another year passed without major battles, during which the British finally put down the Sepoy Rebellion in India. They would no longer be splitting their forces between two theaters of war, meaning that many more British forces could be committed to China. More unfortunate for China still was that a new offensive was organized by Sir Colin Campbell, a veteran of the First Opium War who knew how to supply men to avoid attrition from diseases and weather.

Third Battle of Taku Forts

The Chinese victory was fleeting, and on August 12, 1860, a force of almost twenty thousand Anglo-French soldiers arrived to take the forts which had been reinforced with only about seven thousand men. Instead of attacking by water, the army disembarked to the north and advanced on the forts by land.

After eight days of slowly approaching and building batteries of artillery, the allied forces attacked on the morning of the 20th. Without the logistical nightmare of low tide, the alliance was able to make headway against the defenders, if only barely.

Anglo-French artillery bombed the Chinese guns into uselessness from afar, then the infantry and cavalry began a frontal assault of the four major forts they had eyes on. They fought for every step they took, having to wade through muddy or flooded land while dealing with trenches and spiked barriers made out of bamboo by the Qing defenders.

The battlefield was so hostile to the attackers that they might have gotten bogged down and forced to retreat again, if not for the help of very unlikely allies.

Even as Europeans pushed deeper in to China, anti-Manchu sentiment among the Han and other ethnic groups of China remained strong. It only needed an outlet, and a final, decisive battle against the Qing turned out to be the perfect opportunity. So the Anglo-French assault was joined by unknown thousands of South Chinese laborers and peasants— the people who had suffered the longest under bandits, rebels, taxes, and corrupt Qing officials.

They helped the allies using their knowledge of the land and earthworks, clearing spikes and palisades or wading through flooded trenches in water that came up to their necks. All the while, they remained cool under heavy fire. When the infantry columns reached the forts, it was the Chinese rebels who carried giant ladders up to the walls, or lay them down as bridges for their temporary allies to walk across.

When the battle got its bloodiest in close-quarters around the forts, the Chinese engaged the Qing with no real weapons to speak of. They bravely dived into melee combat with nothing but bamboo sticks. Thanks in part to their rebellion, the Anglo-French won the following day with little more than two hundred casualties, ending the third and final Battle of Taku Forts.

The Europeans were greatly impressed by them and their conduct, and spoke highly of them in accounts of the battle, albeit while referring to them with the disparaging term "coolies."

The Road to Peking

After the Taku Forts fell, the rest of the river forts all the way up to Tianjin surrendered to the Europeans by September 1st. A direct route to the imperial capital was finally open, and with it the end of the war was in sight. The allies either had to take Peking, or threaten the emperor enough that they didn't need to. They opted for diplomacy one last time, with Hong Kong consul Harry Parkes—partial instigator of the Second Opium War—leading the British delegation.

Parkes initially stopped at Tianjin. But the same way that negotiations were stalled two years earlier, the Chinese diplomats whom they met with did not have the unrestricted power to act as they saw fit in the interest of the empire. So

Parkes and company moved ahead of French and British forces to the city of Tungchow—modern Tongzhuo. Here, Parkes managed to secure an agreement to begin negotiating with the appropriate authorities.

But while he was inspecting the future sight of the talks, Parkes was angered to see Qing forces setting camp uncomfortably close by. He complained to the Chinese officials and managed to insult them. At that point, communication broke down. Parkes attempted to flee to alert the approaching Anglo-French column. Parkes and the entire delegation were arrested by order of Sengge Rinchen. They were shipped to Peking on September 18th, where they were imprisoned and interrogated as spies.

The Europeans responded to the diplomatic insult with military force. Their army arrived just outside of Peking on September 21st, separated from the city by the Tonghui River. The final battle of the Second Opium War commenced as ten thousand Anglo-French tried to cross the Palikao bridge guarded by Sengge Rinchen and fifty thousand men.

European infantry advanced on the bridge under the cover of artillery fire with flanking support from cavalry, while Qing forces struggled to get into range. Sengge Rinchen's personal contingent of elite Mongol cavalry tried to break the enemy lines several times with frontal charges, but the concentrated gunfire offered by the average western soldier tore through their horses and armor. The defense was crushed, and Peking was left open to occupation.

The War Ends

Seeing the loss of his army, the Xianfeng Emperor fled the city for a mountain hideout hundreds of kilometers to the northeast, leaving his younger brother Prince Gong to deal with the foreigners at their doorstep. At first, peace talks centered around the release of diplomatic prisoners.

The British Lord Elgin wanted Consul Parkes and his group returned, while Prince Gong was trying to persuade or force Parkes in to intervening in talks on China's behalf if he was released. The argument went back and forth for almost a month, when Prince Gong finally ordered the release of the prisoners on October 18th—those who were still alive, that is.

Most of the delegation had been tortured for information during their stay in Peking, and nearly half of them had died from illness or mistreatment. Many had been put to death by "slow cutting," also known as "death by a thousand cuts."

It was a torturous method of execution that left the bodies of the delegates mutilated beyond recognition when the allies came to collect them. Parkes almost died for the war he started, but his release came just a few days before the Xianfeng Emperor's order to have him executed came down from the mountains.

This softened the blow to British pride, but only barely. It was still very much the *Nerbudda* Incident of the Second Opium War: an ugly act of vengeance against prisoners that would only hurt China more.

The British were livid, and as revenge Lord Elgin ordered the allies to loot and destroy one of the palace complexes in Peking. At first they considered the Forbidden City—the four hundred year old seat of the Chinese emperor and one of the most important landmarks in the entire nation—but eventually they settled on the "least objectionable" option of the emperor's summer palaces.

Peking wasn't formally occupied by the French and British, but it was clear the city was completely at their mercy.

Acting as regent, Prince Gong agreed to ratify the years-old Treaty of Tianjin.

Chapter Six

Aftermath

The Convention of Peking

The Treaty was signed, meaning that several cities including Tianjin were opened to trade and European embassies were established in Peking. But the current peace process wouldn't be as simple as ratifying the Treaty of Tianjin. The European parties pushed for more concessions.

American interests were sated by the Treaty, but the British, French, and Russians sent delegations to further their designs. The British and French teams led by Lord Elgin and Baron Gros pressed Prince Gong hard, and eventually he yielded.

The silver indemnity owed to Britain and France rose from six million total to eight million each. The area of Kowloon was first leased, then officially ceded to Britain as an extension of British Hong Kong. Relatively progressive freedom of religion was established in China, though unsurprisingly the Europeans would use the spread of Christianity to increase their influence on everyday life in the empire.

British ships were given unlimited access to the rivers of China, and a population drain was initiated by allowing them to take indentured Chinese workers overseas to the Americas. Less objectively important, but even more of an insult to the Chinese, all official documents written in Chinese also had to be written in English, and where differences existed between translations, the English version always took precedent.

Not long after, the Russian delegation led by one Nikolay Ignatyev convinced Prince Gong to cede a huge tract of Manchuria in northeast China to the Russian Empire. This was treated as a way to settle the border conflicts the two empires had faced for centuries. This area included part of the ancestral homeland of the Manchus, and was another disgraceful nail in the coffin of the Qing Dynasty in the eyes of their subjects.

But the most damning part of the treaty was yet to come. Britain decided to resolve their trade issues with the China once and for all by altering Chinese law to suit what Britain had been pushing on it for the better part of a century. The opium trade was made legal—not decriminalized, not put in a legal grey area, but legalized—so that it would enjoy all of the protections that other European imports to China now had.

The official end of the Second Opium War was October 24, 1860, when these and other agreements were signed in a ministry building south of the Forbidden City.

The Peking air would have still been tinged by the acrid smoke of the Summer Palaces being burned to the ground nearby. The humiliated emperor-in-exile died in his mountain hideaway a year later.

Post-War China

Remarkably, despite the destruction they wrought on China, the Opium Wars were not the final death knell of the Qing Dynasty. The empire soldiered on for more than fifty years before its dissolution in 1912.

In hindsight, it looks inevitable that the dynasty would fall to rebellions after failing long enough to protect its subjects from foreign and domestic crises.

But at the time, that did not seem to be the case. Resentment was festering in the populace, and the cracks were showing, but there was enough loyalty and stability remaining that it seemed like things could be turned around.

The Tonzghi Reforms, aka Self-Strengthening Movement, which followed immediately after the Opium Wars is very symbolic of that last hurrah. Prince Gong did not become emperor after his older brother's death, but he did become an important adviser to the new Tongzhi Emperor, his nephew, for years to come.

Through the child emperor he was able to begin a series of reforms that intended to partially westernize China. By adapting European technologies and techniques to Chinese life, the movement was meant to strengthen China against foreign powers while also preserving and reinforcing its traditional culture and Confucian worldview.

The reforms lay the groundwork for a modernized China in the twentieth century, but the Qing Dynasty would not live to see them bear fruit before successive rebellions by dissatisfied subjects turned in to a proper revolution.

The final Qing monarch, Empress Dowager Longyu, abdicated the throne alongside her five year-old adopted son, Puyi, in 1911.

But just like the transference of power from one dynasty to another for thousands of years of Chinese history, the Republican and later Communist periods to come would build off of the lessons and accomplishments of the Qing.

The modern state of China has been grappling with the effects of the Opium Wars right up to the current day, such as the return of Hong Kong to Chinese sovereignty in 1997, and the question of whether or not to fully integrate it.

The Future of Opium

Opium use, unfortunately, was not something that died with the Qing. Forced legalization of the drug normalized its usage across all walks of life in China for generations to come. At times, it even became a necessity of life.

After the widespread economic destruction of wars like the Taiping Rebellion, poor farmers had nothing to survive on, and turned to growing poppies. The plant was desired and could be grown in almost any climate and soil quality, so it was easy and reliable to farm.

The Chinese government continued to make weak attempts at suppressing opium, but by the 1880s, even the most anti-opium officials in government eventually had to learn to tacitly accept tax money that only existed thanks to the opium market.

Reportedly, all one needed to do was rip up a few opium stalks at the edge of their field and lay them beside the road to give the illusion of cutting down on the drug to any government workers passing by, and that was enough.

Poppy farming grew so popular in China in fact, that domestic production started to overshadow the imports from European colonies. Within forty years of the conclusion of the Opium Wars, British opium merchants were being driven out of Chinese ports by low homegrown prices that they just couldn't compete with—a last twist of irony that would be hilarious, if it weren't so tragic. When a renewed crackdown on opium came from the government in 1901, it was not European merchants who fought against it, but the people of China themselves.

After the Qing Dynasty crumbled, China became an unstable Republic from 1912 to 1949. The country was plagued by warlords and political parties vying for power during this time, and most factions helped finance themselves with opium money. Addicts numbered in the millions.

It wasn't until the aggressive social policies of Mao Zedong in the 1950s, that the first real progress was made to curb opium production and consumption. Those millions of addicts were forced into rehabilitation, dealers were punished severely and even executed, and opium farms were forced to start growing other crops.

The market shrank, but it survived. Most of the poppy growing moved across the Chinese border in to Southeast Asia, where high numbers of American soldiers would later become addicted to opium during the Vietnam War.

Today, the drug continues to be a source of international hardships.

Thanks to modern pharmaceutical technology, newer and stronger opioids have been created from it, and poppy farming is still a profession around the world.

Conclusion

Simply put, the Opium Wars were a man-made tragedy on a massive scale. Tens of thousands of people died directly because of violence, while uncounted millions of lives were ruined by addiction, disease, starvation, and displacement.

Echoes of the Chinese opium trade can still be felt in the modern narcotic trade. The greed that brought opium to China is as much to blame as the effects of the drug itself.

The wars showed that not even a powerful, sovereign nation thousands of years old was safe from European colonization. They showed that imperialism takes many forms, targeted not just at controlling land or owning the people who live on it, but also at undermining foreign and domestic policy under the pretense of promoting common good- a practice that still exists in the world today.

The Opium Wars also led to the dissolution of the last Chinese empire. Though they didn't hammer the final nail into the Qing Dynasty's coffin, they would damage the government too much to ever recover.

That series of events also thrust China into the technologically advanced, interconnected world that we live in today, and the country has become a huge powerhouse once more.

Above all else, the wars mark a massive turning-point in the history of Asia, and the world at large.

It is impossible to imagine what the world might have been like without these events, for better or for worse.

References

Schiff, Paul L. Jr. "Opium and Its Alkaloids," *American Journal of Pharmaceutical Education*. Vol. 66, No. 2. American Association of Colleges of Pharmacy. 2002. http://archive.ajpe.org/legacy/ajpe_metaview.asp?ID=900

Ebrey, Patricia B. *Chinese Civilization: A Sourcebook*. Free Press. 1993. Print.

Zheng, Yangwen. "The Social Life of Opium in China, 1483-1999." *Modern Asian Studies*, Vol. 37, No. 1, 2003. JSTOR, www.jstor.org/stable/3876550

Fairbank, John K. *The Cambridge History of China*, Volume 10: Late Ch'ing, 1800-1911, Part 1. Cambridge University Press. 1978. Print.

Brewster, David. *The Edinburgh Encyclopædia*, Volume 11. J. and E. Parker, Northwestern University. 1832. https://books.google.com/books?id=cg4bAQAAMAAJ

Garner, Richard L. "Long-Term Silver Mining Trends in Spanish America: A Comparative Analysis of Peru and Mexico." *The American Historical Review*, vol. 93, no. 4, 1988. JSTOR, www.jstor.org/stable/1863529

Schottenhammer, Angela. *The East Asian Maritime World 1400–1800: Its Fabrics of Power and Dynamics of Exchanges*. East Asian Maritime History 4. Harrassowitz Verlag, Wiesbaden. 2007.

Elleman, Bruce A. *Modern Chinese Warfare, 1795-1989*. Taylor & Francis, New York. 2001.

McNeil, William H., Mitsuko Iriye, editors. *Modern Asia and Africa, Readings in World History*, Vol. 9. Oxford University Press. 1971. https://sourcebooks.fordham.edu/mod/1839lin2.asp

Backhouse, E, J. O. P. Bland. *Annals and Memoirs of the Court of Peking*. Houghton Mifflin. 1914. https://china.usc.edu/emperor-qianlong-letter-george-iii-1793

Eitel, E. J. *Europe in China: The History of Hong Kong from the Beginning to the Year 1882*. Luzac & Company, London. 1895. Internet Archive. Retrieved 24 June 2019. https://archive.org/details/europeinchinahis00eiteuoft

Hanes, W. Travis III, Frank Sanello. *Opium Wars: The Addiction of One Empire and the Corruption of Another*. Sourcebooks, Inc. 2004.

British Parliament. *Correspondence Relating to China*. T.R. Harrison, London. 1840. Internet Archive. Retrieved 26 June 2019. https://archive.org/details/CorrespondenceRelatingToChina1840

Morse, Hosea B. *The International Relations of the Chinese Empire*. Vol 1. Paragon Book Gallery, New York. 1910. Internet Archive. https://archive.org/details/internationalrel01mors

Janin, Hunt. *The India–China Opium Trade in the Nineteenth Century*. McFarland. 1999.

Rubin, Alfred P. "The Sino-Indian Border Disputes." *The International and Comparative Law Quarterly*, vol. 9, no. 1, 1960. JSTOR. www.jstor.org/stable/756256

Andrade, Tonio. *The Gunpowder Age: China, Military Innovation, and the Rise of the West in World History*. Princeton University Press. 2016.

Haijian, Mao (2016-10-18). *The Qing Empire and the Opium War*. Cambridge University Press.

Fay, Peter Ward. *The Opium War, 1840–1842*. University of North Carolina Press. 2000.

Hummel, Arthur William (1943). *Eminent Chinese of the Ch'ing Period (1644–1912)*. United States Government Printing Office. http://www.dartmouth.edu/~qing/WEB/

Paine, Lincoln P. *Warships of the World to 1900*. Houghton Mifflin Harcourt. 2000.

McPherson, Duncan; Carruthers, Bob. *The First Opium War, The Chinese Expedition 1840–1842, The Illustrated Edition*. Coda Books Ltd. 2013.

Dillon, Michael. *China: A Modern History*. I. B. Tauris. 2010.

Glenn Melancon, "Honor in Opium? The British Declaration of War on China, 1839–1840." *International History Review*, *x*xi, no 4. 1999.

Bingham, John Elliot. *Narrative of the Expedition to China*. 2nd Edition. Volume 2. Henry Colburn. 1843.
https://books.google.com/books/about/Narrative_of_the_Expedition_to_China.html?id=8TGwqgOCFR0C

Bernard, William Dallas; Hall, William Hutcheon (1847). The Nemesis in China (3rd ed.). London: Henry Colburn.

Perdue, Peter C., The First Opium War: The Anglo Chinese War of 1839-1842 (PDF), Visualizing Cultures at the Massachusetts Institute of Technology.
https://visualizingcultures.mit.edu/opium_wars_01/ow1_essay.pdf

Wakeman, Frederic E. *Strangers at the Gate: Social Disorder in South China, 1839-1861*. University of California Press. 1997.
https://books.google.com/books?id=NCgXTcXH-3MC

Rait, Robert S. *The Life and Campaigns of Hugh, First Viscount Gough, Field-Marshal*. Volume 1. Westminster: Archibald Constable. 1903.
https://books.google.com/books/about/The_life_and_campaigns_of_Hugh_first_Vis.html?id=pR5GAQAAIAAJ

Paget, William H. *Frontier and Overseas Expeditions From India*. Volume 6. India Army Intelligence Branch. 1907. Internet Archive.
https://archive.org/details/frontieroverseas03indi/page/n8

Waley, Arthur. *The Opium War Through Chinese Eyes*. Taylor & Francis. 2013. First published 1958.

University of Michigan. "Bulletins and Other State Intelligence." F. Watts. 1841.

https://books.google.com/books/about/Bulletins_and_Other_State_Intelligence_C.html?id=ZMQsAAAAMAAJ

Publishing, D. K. (1 October 2009). *War: The Definitive Visual History*. Penguin. 2009.

Granville G. Loch. *The Closing Events of the Campaign in China: The Operations in the Yang-tze-kiang and Treaty of Nanking*. London. 1843. Internet Archive. https://archive.org/details/bub_gb_F_eyJPTERisC

Bate, H. Maclear. *Reports from Formosa*. E. P. Dutton. 1952.

"The Treaty of Nanjing," https://en.wikisource.org/wiki/Treaty_of_Nanking

Wang, Dong. *China's Unequal Treaties: Narrating National History*. Lexington Books. 2005.

Edward J. M. Rhoads. *Manchus & Han: Ethnic Relations and Political Power in Late Qing and Early Republican China, 1861-1928*. University of Washington Press. 2000. https://www.jstor.org/stable/j.ctvbtzm6b

Platt, Stephen R. *Autumn in the Heavenly Kingdom: China, the West, and the Epic Story of the Taiping Civil War*. Knopf. 2012.

Franz H. Michael, ed. *The Taiping Rebellion: History and Documents*. University of Washington Press. 1966.

Spence, Jonathan D. *God's Chinese Son: The Taiping Heavenly Kingdom of Hong Xiuquan*. W.W. Norton. 1996.

D'Aguilar, George Charles. *Correspondence Relative to the Operations in the Canton River*. Arthur Wallis. 1847. https://books.google.com/books/about/Correspondence_relative_to_the_Operation.html?id=fRthAAAAcAAJ

Bard, Solomon. *Voices from the Past: Hong Kong 1842-1918*. Hong Kong University Press. 2002.

Lovell, Julia. *Opium War: Drugs, Dreams and the Making of China*. Picador. 2011.

Fairbank, John King. Trade and Diplomacy on the China Coast: The Opening of the Treaty Ports, 1842-1854. Volume 1. Harvard University Press. 1953.

Porter, Maj Gen Whitworth. *History of the Corps of Royal Engineers* Vol I. The Institution of Royal Engineers. 1889. https://archive.org/details/historycorpsroy00watsgoog

David, Saul. Victoria's Wars: The Rise of Empire. Penguin Books. 2007.

Wong, J. Y. *Deadly Dreams: Opium and the Arrow War (1856-1860) in China*. Cambridge University Press. 2002.

Elleman, Bruce A. *Naval Coalition Warfare: From the Napoleonic War to Operation Iraqi Freedom*. Routledge. 2008.

Wang, Dong. China's Unequal Treaties: Narrating National History. Lexington Books. 2005.

Fang, Chao-ying (1943). "Ch'i-ying (Kiying)." In Hummel Sr., Arthur W. (ed.). Eminent Chinese of the Ch'ing Period. 1. United States Government Printing Office.

Bruce, James; et al. *Peace Treaty between the Queen of Great Britain and the Emperor of China, Tianjin*. 1858. https://en.wikisource.org/wiki/Treaty_of_Tien-Tsin_between_the_Queen_of_Great_Britain_and_the_Emperor_of_China

Hsü, Immanuel C. Y. *The Rise of Modern China*. Oxford University Press. 2000.

Greenwood, Adrian (2015). Victoria's Scottish Lion: The Life of Colin Campbell, Lord Clyde. UK: History Press.

China: Being a Military Report on the North-eastern Portions of the Provinces of Chih-li and Shan-tung, Nanking and Its Approaches, Canton and Its Approaches. Government Central Branch Press. 1884. https://books.google.com/books?id=O1AMAQAAMAAJ&pg=PA28#v=onepage&q&f=false

Chisholm, Hugh, ed. "Parkes, Sir Harry Smith." Encyclopædia Britannica. Volume 20. 11th ed. Cambridge University Press. 1911.

https://en.wikisource.org/wiki/1911_Encyclop%C3%A6dia_Britannica/Parkes,_Sir_Harry_Smith

Boulger, Demetrius Charles. *China*. Kessinger Publishing. 1893. http://www.gutenberg.org/cache/epub/6708/pg6708.html

Endacott, G. B.; Carroll, John M. *A Biographical Sketch-book of Early Hong Kong*. Hong Kong University Press. 2005.

Harris, David; Van Slyke, Lyman P. *Of Battle and Beauty: Felice Beato's Photographs of China*. University of California Press. 1999.

Liu, Kwang-Ching; Chu, Samuel C. *Liu Hung-Chang and China's Early Modernization*. Routledge. 2016.

Spence, Jonathan. "Opium Smoking in Ch'ing China." *Conflict and Control in Late Imperial China*. University of California Press. 1975.

Spence, Jonathan D. *The Search for Modern China*. Norton. 2013.

Edward R. Slack. *Opium, State, and Society: China's Narco-Economy and the Guomindang, 1924–1937*. University of Hawaii Press. 2001.

About History Compacted

Here in History Compacted, we see history as a large collection of stories. Each of these amazing stories of the past can help spark ideas for the future. However, history is often proceeded as boring and incomprehensible. That is why it is our mission to simplify the fascinating stories of history.

Follow History Compacted:

Website: www.historycompacted.com

Twitter: @HistoryCompact

Facebook: https://www.facebook.com/historycompacted/

Instagram: @history_compacted

Dark Minds In History

For updates about new releases, as well as exclusive promotions, sign up for our newsletter and you can also receive a free book today. Thank you and see you soon.

Sign up here: http://bit.ly/2ToHti3

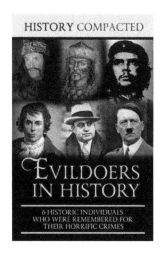

Evildoers in History: 6 Historic Individuals Remembered For Their Horrific Crimes is a book that explores the stories of six infamous criminals in history, these evildoers were not remembered by their countless murders but by the brutality with which they took the lives of their victims. There is no other term to describe them but ruthless, as you will soon find out.

Prepare yourself, the gruesome part of history is not for everyone...

Pg
36
41
94

112
120

1) Opium
2) Morphine
3) Heroine